THE MINDSET EQUATION

THE ART OF LIVING IN ABUNDANCE

SARA KISSING

Copyright © Sara Kissing 2023

All rights reserved. No part of this publication may be reproduced, distributed, or transmitted in any form or by any means, including photocopying, recording, or other electronic or mechanical methods, without the author's prior written permission, except in the case of brief quotations embodied in critical reviews and certain other non-commercial uses permitted by copyright law.

The author of this book does not dispense medical advice or prescribe the use of any technique as a form of treatment for physical, emotional, or medical problems without the advice of a physician, either directly or indirectly. The intent of the author is only to offer general information to help you in your quest for emotional, physical, and spiritual well-being. In the event you use any of the information in this book for yourself, the author and the publisher assume no responsibility for your actions. For permission requests, please get in touch with the author.

Hardcover ISBN: 978-1-959898-99-3
E-book ISBN: 979-8-9864805-5-8
Paperback ISBN: 979-8-9864805-6-5

This book is dedicated to my daughter Kamira.

I am forever grateful for the unconditional love that flows between us. You are my inspiration, and I am forever grateful to have you in my life. Keep manifesting your dreams, and let the butterflies guide your path.

MiMa Power

TABLE OF CONTENTS

INSIDE THE PAGES: HOW TO USE THIS BOOK		1
INTRODUCTION		7

PART ONE: TRANSFORMING YOUR MINDSET

CHAPTER 1	YOUR JOURNAL	25
CHAPTER 2	INTERCONNECTEDNESS	29
CHAPTER 3	A POSITIVE MINDSET	35
CHAPTER 4	GRATITUDE	43
CHAPTER 5	PRIMING	49
CHAPTER 6	THE HAPPY STATE	53
CHAPTER 7	MINDFULNESS	61
CHAPTER 8	MEDITATION	65
CHAPTER 9	LOVE YOURSELF FIRST	73
CHAPTER 10	THE HAPPY POWER HOUR	79
CHAPTER 11	NOURISH & MOVE	85
CHAPTER 12	YOUR PEERS	91

PART TWO: SETTING GOALS AND THE LAW OF ATTRACTION

CHAPTER 13	ENERGETIC VIBRATIONS	101
CHAPTER 14	DREAM BIG	109
CHAPTER 15	GOAL SETTING	115
CHAPTER 16	LIMITING BELIEFS VS EMPOWERING BELIEFS	123
CHAPTER 17	THE LAW OF ATTRACTION	133
CHAPTER 18	MANIFESTING AND VISUALIZATION	145
CHAPTER 19	AFFIRMATIONS AND INCANTATIONS	151

PART THREE: GOOD KARMA AND GIVING BACK

CHAPTER 20	SYNCHRONICITIES	161
CHAPTER 21	EASY IS RIGHT AND RIGHT IS EASY	169
CHAPTER 22	KARMA OR CAUSE AND EFFECT	175
CHAPTER 23	GIVING BACK AND CONTRIBUTION	181
CHAPTER 24	THE 10 DAY POSITIVE MINDSET TRANSFORMATION	187

SUGGESTED READING	205
ACKNOWLEDGEMENTS	209
ABOUT THE AUTHOR	211
SAMPLE AFFIRMATIONS	213

"THE PURPOSE OF
 OUR LIVES IS
 TO BE HAPPY."

DALAI LAMA

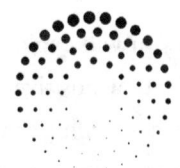

INSIDE THE PAGES: HOW TO USE THIS BOOK

Welcome to an empowering journey where you'll unlock the potential of your positive mindset, manifest your dreams, and sustain the momentum of happiness. This book is divided into three sections:

Part One	Transforming Your Mindset
Part Two	Setting Goals and The Law of Attraction
Part Three	Good Karma and Giving Back

In each chapter, you will find a thorough exploration of a specific topic, accompanied by practical steps to apply the knowledge you gain. The chapters are intentionally designed to be short and to the point, considering that the typical adult attention span ranges from 10 to 25 minutes, according to studies. This ensures that each chapter delivers valuable insights and tools concisely, allowing you to absorb the information effectively.

Whether you choose to read the book cover to cover or selectively explore the chapters that resonate with you, you can expect a focused and impactful reading experience that supports your journey of self-discovery and transformation. Embrace the power of a positive mindset; take inspired action, and watch, as your dreams become a reality.

Part One: Transforming Your Mindset

In the first part of this book, you will explore the essential tools and practices that will help you cultivate a positive mindset. Each chapter is designed to guide you through a specific technique or approach that will shift your perspective, elevate your energy, and empower you to embrace a more optimistic outlook. From the teachings of gratitude and the art of meditation to the power of priming techniques and self-care practices, you will discover a wealth of strategies to transform your mindset and unlock your true potential.

Once you have diligently worked through the first chapters of this book, something remarkable happens. Not only do you experience a profound shift in your perspective and overall well-being, but you also begin to vibrate on a higher positive energy and frequency. This elevated state of being is crucial because it allows you to tap into the immense power of the Law of Attraction. The Law of Attraction states that like attracts like, meaning that the energy you emit into the Universe attracts similar energy back to you. When you are positive and radiating joy, you naturally draw positive experiences, opportunities, and people into your life.

By cultivating a positive mindset through the tools and practices outlined in this book, you align yourself with the frequency of abundance, success, and fulfillment. This alignment enables you to effortlessly attract the very things you desire and manifest your dreams into reality.

Imagine a magnet that effortlessly attracts metal objects. Similarly, when you are in a state of happiness and positivity, you become a magnet for all the wonderful things the Universe offers. Your elevated energy vibration acts as a powerful beacon, attracting opportunities, synchronicities, and serendipitous events that align with your desires. It's important to note that the Law of Attraction is not a magic wand that instantly grants your every wish. It requires consistent effort, belief, and inspired action. However, by harnessing the power of a positive mindset and aligning yourself with the frequency of happiness and positivity, you create the ideal conditions for the Law of Attraction to work in your favor.

Part Two: Setting Goals and The Law of Attraction

As you continue your journey, you will uncover the exciting possibilities that arise from your newly transformed mindset and elevated energy frequency. This section of the book explains the vibrational energies that are at play, and it guides you in setting your goals and discovering your dreams. It provides tools to overcome any limiting beliefs that may hinder your faith and belief in achieving them. With your positive mindset and newfound energy, you will embark on a journey of self-exploration to uncover your deepest desires and aspirations.

You will find techniques and exercises to help you clarify your goals and gain clarity on what you truly want in life. You can set a clear path towards their manifestation by identifying and understanding your dreams. One of the key tools explored in this part is the Law of Attraction. You will learn how to harness this universal principle to your advantage. You will discover how to align your thoughts, emotions, and actions with your desired outcomes through visualization techniques, manifestation practices, and affirmations. These tools will empower you to attract and manifest the experiences, opportunities, and abundance that align with your dreams and goals. This process allows you to cultivate unwavering faith and belief in your ability to create the life you truly desire. Engaging with these practices will unlock your full potential and create a life filled with abundance, joy, and fulfillment.

Part Three: Good Karma and Giving Back

As your mindset shifts and your dreams begin to materialize, you will experience a beautiful tapestry of synchronicities in your life. In the final part of this book, we will explore the meaningful coincidences and serendipitous events that occur when you align with your true purpose.

As you witness the transformation of your mindset and the manifestation of your dreams, you will experience a ripple effect of positive change and good karma in your own life and the lives of those around you. Together, we will delve into the concept of giving back and making a meaningful contribution to the world. As you embrace your newfound abundance, you will be inspired to share your unique gifts with others. By working with the tools provided in this book, you will discover that once your desires manifest, you will feel a deep urge to give back. You will expore various ways to contribute, help others, and positively impact both people and the planet. You will have the power to bring about positive change and transformation in the world around you.

THE STRUCTURE OF THIS BOOK:

- Chapter Length:
  The chapters are deliberately crafted to be concise and focused, considering the average adult attention span of 10 to 25 minutes. This approach ensures that each chapter delivers valuable insights and tools effectively, allowing you to absorb the information efficiently.

- Action Items:
  By promptly practicing and applying what you learn, you accelerate your mastery and cultivate enduring habits. Theoretical learning formats that solely provide knowledge without application are ineffective in teaching you how to utilize what you have learned. Throughout this book, you will be motivated to consistently apply, practice, and derive benefits from your newfound knowledge, leading to measurable growth at every step.

- 10-Day Positive Mindset Transformation:
  At the conclusion of the book, you will uncover the transformative "10-Day Positive Mindset Transformation." This guide serves as a practical manual, providing you

with actionable steps and a daily checklist to effectively apply the tools presented in this book and cultivate new positive habits. It follows a micro-application format, allowing you to incorporate these practices into your daily routine and experience meaningful change.

"WE ARE HERE TO
AWAKEN FROM OUR
ILLUSION OF
SEPARATENESS."

THICH NHAT HANH

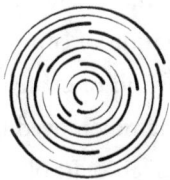

INTRODUCTION

Beneath my high school yearbook photo, the caption reads, *"Could the witch kindly leave the premises?" Sara, a treasure trove of humor.*

In high school, my friends affectionately called me the 'good witch,' a label that still resonates with me even after three decades. To this day, it holds a special place in my heart, symbolized by the silver magic wand hanging from my rearview mirror. It serves as a reminder of the magic that permeates our world.

Ever since childhood, I've preferred happiness over sadness, consistently brightening others' days with humor and a cheerful disposition. It was my way of coping with the challenges life threw my way. While my early years were tough, they were also filled with extraordinary experiences that seemed almost magical. Looking back, I now understand that it wasn't magic but the Universe aligning my desires with reality.

Manifesting and visualizing my dreams played a significant role in my life, although I didn't fully grasp what I was doing until my early forties. Before that, concepts like the Law of Attraction, manifestation, karma, and energetic alignment were foreign to me. I didn't understand the importance of balancing positive and negative thoughts, nor did I realize that maintaining a positive mindset is a choice that requires daily effort.

My optimistic outlook has played a pivotal role in achieving numerous extraordinary goals throughout my journey. However, it's essential to acknowledge that my limited understanding of the Law of Attraction has sometimes led to the manifestation of complex challenges.

My childhood was a whirlwind of change and unpredictability. Raised in a multicultural setting, my family moved frequently, but the most significant shift occurred when I was ten years old as we relocated from Germany to Texas. It was pure bliss, and this time stands out as the happiest phase of my early years, sparking an enduring passion for the United States right from day one.

At twelve, a pivotal moment arrived when my parents split, forcing me to leave Texas and abandon my American dream. I ended up at my grandmother's while my parents moved on. This marked the start of my penchant for daydreaming and maintaining journals during my teenage years. The walls of my room were covered in posters and magazine clippings, creating an extensive vision board. These practices served as a means of coping and, unbeknownst to me then, played a role in manifesting my desires. Only now do I comprehend I was inadvertently harnessing the principles of the Law of Attraction. During my high school years, I consistently shared with my friends my unwavering desire to return to the United States and pursue art studies at a university. Despite my family not intending to fund this costly endeavor, my determination remained unwavering for years.

After graduation, I embarked on a quest to live and study abroad. It proved to be a very complex and costly endeavor, and I often felt like success was beyond my reach. Discouraged, I enrolled in a local university in Germany. I was only enrolled for 2 months when my life finally took a turn for the better. I had to take up a job as a bartender, and that's where I met Chris, who worked at the same bar to save for his upcoming studies in the United States. We began dating, and Chris became my guiding light, showing me how to fulfill my dream. Yet, I still faced the obstacle of expensive international tuition fees that I couldn't afford.

After three months, it looked like our relationship would come to an end, as Chris's departure was getting closer. He was invited to a dinner party a week before leaving for Texas. I tagged along, and Chris's friend introduced me to Michael, who immediately shared his woes about his recent divorce and his newfound custody of his young boys. He was in anguish as he had to relocate to Texas within two weeks for a promotion. He needed a German and English-speaking au pair as soon as possible. I couldn't stop smiling. My destiny was sealed.

Only two weeks later, Chris and I moved to Texas. I truly manifested one of my biggest dreams, and I didn't even know I was doing it. I had a positive mindset; I truly believed I could study abroad. I used the tools of manifesting, visualization, and journaling—the Universe then orchestrated the amazing synchronicities that let my way.

I was filled with happiness, successfully obtained multiple scholarships, and never had to worry about covering my expenses. However, after four adventurous years, our visions for the future no longer aligned, and I discovered he had met someone else. It was during this time that the Law of Attraction seemed to unfold in the opposite direction.

For weeks on end, my mind was consumed by one thing. I felt utterly miserable and feared that my dream was slipping away. This subconscious focus on negativity inadvertently manifested the worst outcome imaginable. All my energy was directed towards my suffering, and as a result, I unintentionally attracted more negativity into my life. Looking back, I wish someone had enlightened me about the power of choice, even during the darkest hours. I now understand that I could choose happiness and maintain a positive mindset, regardless of the circumstances.

We all have the power to decide whether to delve into a negative spiral or hold our heads high, focusing on the positive aspects of life despite the challenges we may face. We are the masters of our thoughts, and no one else controls them. Life will always present obstacles, and change is inevitable. However, how we approach each day and confront these challenges is our choice.

Consequently, my health began deteriorating, manifesting as sickness, panic attacks, and a nervous rash. In an attempt to heal and recover, I spent the summer break in Germany, seeking solace. Upon arriving in Germany, my body reached its breaking point, leading me to make the difficult choice to stay there once again.

The Law of Attraction is an ever-present force, shaping our life experiences regardless of our background or location. It operates through the power of our thoughts. Each thought we have emits energy that attracts similar experiences into our lives.

I experienced this firsthand, serving as a living example of its influence. I was completely unaware that I was unintentionally inviting chaos into my life. In my perception, I saw myself as a victim, manipulated by external forces. However, the truth was that I held power and control over my own life like a puppeteer pulling all the strings.

I stayed in Germany and quickly accepted my destiny. Upon completing my Master's degree, I regained a sense of alignment. During this period, thoughts of returning to the United States started to occupy my mind again. My heart yearned to be back in the U.S., and alongside this longing, I found myself daydreaming about my future spouse, fueled by a strong desire to build a family of my own.

One evening, I visited a friend who had recently returned from a trip to New York. As he shared his vacation photos, I stumbled upon a picture of a guy named Sebastian. Instantly, I exclaimed, "Who is this? Because I strongly feel he's the man I'm destined to marry." My friend burst into laughter, thinking I was joking, but I was completely serious. All I could think about was finding a way to meet this man. Of course, just two weeks later, I received an invitation to a barbecue, and Sebastian was there. It was love at first sight for both of us.

As I was joyfully driving to a date with him, a powerful intuition washed over me, foretelling that I would have a daughter with him. In my mind, I had already chosen the name Kamira for her, a name that had lingered in my thoughts for years, and I crafted vivid mental images again and clung to them like enchanting fairy tales.

After just two months of dating, Sebastian and I decided to move in together. Our friends loved being around us because our happiness was infectious. While on a girls' vacation, one of them asked me if Sebastian was "the one." I confidently replied, "Yes, this is the man I am going to marry on a beautiful beach, barefoot in my wedding dress, somewhere exotic." One of my friends said, "Yes, she has been saying that since high school." the others just laughed in disbelief.

As it turns out, the Law of Attraction governs our lives every day, whether we are aware of it or not, whether we believe in it or not. A year later, we joyfully exchanged vows on the pristine beach of Rangali Island in the Maldives. With the soft sand beneath my bare feet, I glided down the shoreline in my wedding dress, immersed in pure happiness and shared laughter. Surrounded by our cherished friends and family, the week was a testament to the fulfillment of my visualizations. Another year later, our daughter, Kamira, was born, and we moved our small family to California. I was living my dream again.

Unfortunately, our story did not end with the traditional "Happily ever after." Instead, it all came crashing down once again. Alongside the joys of being married for many years and the immense blessing of having a wonderful daughter, I also experienced the heart-wrenching pain of my divorce and the unique challenges of being a single parent for an extended period. Despite these circumstances, I have successfully navigated through various and extreme financial fluctuations, constantly striving to stay ahead of the game. I remained oblivious to the extent to which I unknowingly attracted and influenced the constant, extreme changes that seemed to permeate my life. It felt like a never-ending roller coaster ride, with its ups and downs, twists and turns.

Nobody had enlightened me about the possibility that I might have played a significant role in these recurring changes. Instead, repeatedly, I habitually blamed external factors, failing to recognize my participation in this intricate game of life.

When I was in my mid-thirties, finally my first breakthrough moment arrived. It was during my divorce in 2006. While outwardly maintaining a composed demeanor to keep my four-year-old daughter happy, I was silently screaming for help internally. My thoughts were focused on getting answers. "What do I have to do so that this roller coaster stops? How can I maintain my happiness?" I desperately sought assistance, and again, my plea did not go unheard.

The Universe responded during a trip to Germany for my grandmother's funeral when I had a profound encounter with Viram, a spiritual guru and teacher. Sitting at JFK airport, consumed by sadness, Viram approached me. His deep knowledge of spirituality and personal growth was immediately evident, and this marked the start of my journey to find the answers I'd been seeking. Over the next year, Viram played a crucial role in guiding and supporting my spiritual and personal growth.

I explored yoga, meditation, and mindfulness and explored teachings from spiritual leaders through the resources Viram provided. All focused on inner peace and happiness. Viram's spiritual insights deeply resonated with me as I pursued transformation. His impact on my life is something I'll forever cherish. However, despite his profound influence, I still yearned for more guidance. I had a burning desire to uncover the key to understanding life's forces and transforming my life permanently. It was like searching for a handbook that could illuminate the path to complete fulfillment, happiness, and abundant blessings.

But first, I had to relocate to Germany once again. Following my divorce, my ex-husband was going through a difficult phase, and his actions and the company he kept around our daughter reached a point where her safety was compromised. The day came after a distressing incident that required police involvement. Following the advice of my attorney, I had to depart within a mere 24 hours to ensure my daughter's safety. It meant leaving behind everything, and with just two suitcases packed, I took my daughter and embarked on a new journey.

After an eventful journey back to Germany, I found myself residing with my mother and stepfather, a situation far from ideal. Right from the beginning, I embarked on securing a job and finding a suitable apartment for my daughter and me. It was a very stressful couple of weeks. I drove around the city tirelessly, determined to find the perfect place. Yet, as four weeks elapsed, desperation began to seep in. Despite attending numerous job interviews, none proved successful, and it seemed as though I had inspected every apartment available in the city.

As I was engrossed in yet another online search one evening, a realization struck me. I leaned back and asked myself: "Sara, what is it that you truly want? What is the ultimate outcome you wish to achieve? What is your goal?" I would usually ask my clients or team members those questions when working on solutions.

Over the next hour, I honed in on my desires. I had a crystal-clear vision of the kind of apartment I yearned for, and I made sure to jot it down. My ideal home would be 1200 sq ft, 2/1 space nestled within an old villa in the Westerberg area, perched atop a hill with a picturesque view and a balcony – all within my budget. A smile graced my face, and without hesitation, I placed an ad in the newspaper the following weekend.

That very evening, I also took a moment to pen down my ideal job. I envisioned myself in an upper management role, serving as a creative director leading teams of talented designers within an advertising agency – my passion. I promptly placed another ad in the newspaper.

As soon as the newspaper hit the stands, my phone rang. A warm-hearted woman was on the other end, sharing details about their apartment located in the Westerberg area, nestled within an old villa. Within a mere hour of our conversation, I met with her. To my delight, the apartment matched my vision perfectly.

Remarkably, on that very same day, the founder of a well-established advertising agency contacted me. I was invited to a job interview, and a week later, I joyfully accepted the job as their new creative director.

It was not until I committed to sit down and intentionally define my goals, writing down every detail, that I witnessed the remarkable manifestation of the apartment and the job. At that moment, I remained oblivious to the powerful forces at work; I took action and allowed the enchantment to unfold.

We were really happy in our new home. My daughter was safe and joyous, and I even started practicing yoga and meditation again. Once again, I accepted my situation. And only the quest to find out how to keep my dreams alive had not been quenched. As the years passed, I wholeheartedly embraced the role of a single mother by choice while simultaneously juggling the demands of my job as a creative director. However, the constant exhaustion from my demanding career began to take its toll, and I found myself on the brink of burnout. Due to my profound fatigue, I subconsciously started reciting a simple phrase, "I just don't want to see it anymore," a common German expression used when one reaches the end of their tether. Little did I realize the profound impact of our daily self-talk, or affirmations, could have on manifesting outcomes.

For weeks, I reluctantly commuted to work, hoping to avoid the demanding situation. My team was under immense pressure, managing multiple key accounts requiring meticulous attention. Then, a health crisis hit. One morning, excruciating pain surged through my right eye. Looking in the mirror, I saw a horrifying sight – my eye was swollen, with red and yellow hues, and my vision was significantly blurred. It was clear I needed immediate medical care.

The diagnosis was grim: a severe case of Uveitis, and the doctor's words were ominous – I had to stop everything to prevent losing my eyesight. This meant a complete two-week halt: no screens, no TV, no iPhone, no emails, no work on design projects, no reading, no sunlight, no exercise, and no driving.

Wearing sunglasses, I felt like I was in a world of peaceful silence. The constant noise of my daily life had suddenly stopped. My friends rallied around and provided support, and humor became my solace. When they visited, we all wore sunglasses, shared smiles and gathered in my kitchen, enjoying wine by candlelight. Having such a strong community of friends was a true blessing.

For two weeks, I lived in near isolation, with only my thoughts and reflection for company. During this time, I revisited books on positive affirmations and began incorporating them into my daily routine. I developed a mental gratitude list and realized the reason behind my ailment. Just before falling ill, I had been introduced to Rhonda Byrne's "The Secret," a self-help book that explores the Law of Attraction. It highlights the power of thoughts and beliefs in shaping reality and attracting desired outcomes. I realized I had inadvertently attracted my illness through the Law of Attraction. Reading the book, I finally understood its power. I had experienced firsthand that the Law worked both ways and my repeated affirmation of "I don't want to see it anymore" had caused my vision issues. I had to consciously reverse my condition by focusing on manifesting my health.

During this self-care period, I gained a newfound clarity about my future. After years of being an "Über-mom," I desired a more traditional motherhood experience. It was time for self-love. I created a fresh list and vision board outlining the life I wanted, which included finding a new partner, returning to the USA with my daughter, and stepping away from my role as a creative director.

One day, a friend surprised me with a gift – a do-it-yourself kit named "Dream-Prince-Play-Doh." The kit's instructions urged me to mold my ideal partner with Play-Doh, all while manifesting his existence. It was a fusion of manifestation and magic. We shared laughter as we crafted my prince, and I added conspicuously long arms, explaining that I desired a partner with exceptional hugging abilities. I also made a list of traits for my partner and added a condition that spotting a butterfly would signify I was on the right path.

In line with my new list, I made space in my closet, leaving empty hangers for my future prince – a manifestation technique I had learned. I placed men's shower gel in my bathroom, a subtle signal to the Universe. Five months later, a man sat beside me while sitting in my chiropractor's office. We struck up a conversation about the United States, and he invited me to breakfast the following week.

As I drove to the café, a car adorned with a massive butterfly sticker led me to my destination. It was my sign. Our first breakfast together revealed that he loved the United States and possessed exceptionally long arms. After several dates, he invited me to his home, where a substantial butterfly painting adorned his living room. It seemed like destiny had intervened.

Interestingly, on his first night at my place, he playfully remarked about the presence of a men's shower gel left behind by my "previous lovers?" I felt a twinge of embarrassment, unable to confess that I had been secretly manifesting his presence in my life. To my surprise, when I spent my first night at his place, I was shocked to find the same shower gel in his bathroom. It was a delightful synchronicity that further deepened our connection. Within just a year, we and my daughter moved (back) to the USA. My energy was vibrant, imbued with love, and everything felt perfect. I was in alignment, living my dream once more.

After my introduction to "The Secret," my life underwent a profound transformation. It all started to make sense. Upon reflecting on my life, it became evident that I had been unconsciously harnessing this power for the past two decades, both for good and bad. I grew deeply intrigued by the concept of sustaining momentum once my dreams became a reality. I couldn't understand why these dreams seemed to slip away repeatedly.

My journey into spiritual growth guided by my guru and enhanced by mindfulness, yoga, and meditation, gave me a glimpse of a greater truth. However, it took another five years, filled with ups and downs, to uncover the key to consistently manifesting these insights.

In my quest for answers, I explored numerous books and consulted with various professionals, including therapists, hypnotists, gurus, life coaches, and astrologers. I also immersed myself in meditation and yoga retreats, actively participated in life transformation workshops, and attended events led by renowned motivational speakers and coaches. I was determined to explore every avenue in my pursuit of understanding and maintaining lasting happiness and fulfillment.

Surprisingly, I found striking similarities in various teachings, ranging from religious doctrines to business success coaching. Everyone I encountered seemed to have valuable advice on the path to true transformation, even though none provided the complete solution.

As time passed, I skillfully assembled the fragments of knowledge I had collected, constructing a comprehensive and meaningful understanding. I realized that success isn't solely defined by moments of triumph but also by how we navigate challenges and transformations along our journey.

I've learned that our new reality quickly becomes our default once we achieve a certain goal or manifest a dream. It becomes our new normal, and we may become complacent, feeling content and secure. However, at this very juncture, we must choose to sustain our happiness. We need to choose a positive mindset and acknowledge the positive changes that have occurred. Just as when embarking on the journey of manifesting our desires, we must initially align ourselves with positive energy and find happiness in the present to harness the power of the Law of Attraction.

Our mental state is a precious treasure. Picture it as a scale. We should aim to maintain a balance where the side filled with positive and happy feelings outweighs the negative daily. While it's natural to experience occasional sadness, anger, or disappointment, it's essential not to dwell on these negative emotions. Acknowledge them briefly, then consciously shift your focus back and tip the scale toward the positive.

How we present ourselves and show up in life each day is of paramount importance. Cultivating a positive mindset, aligning our actions with our goals and values, practicing self-love and gratitude, nurturing our physical well-being, surrounding ourselves with positive influences, and giving back are all vital components for achieving fulfillment, success, and sustaining momentum in our journey.

Within the pages of this book, you will find a comprehensive toolkit organized into three parts, each offering essential tools to 1. Cultivate a positive mindset, 2. Define your goal to harness the Law of Attraction, and 3. Explore ways to sustain happiness and alignment while giving back.

Each section is divided into short, self-contained chapters. While starting at the beginning and progressing linearly is recommended, you can also dive into specific topics that match your current needs. The action steps in this book may appear repetitive sometimes, but they are intentionally designed to be interconnected. These steps serve as a guide for you to practice and apply what you learn immediately. Doing so lets you master the material more quickly and develop it into a lasting habit.

> Transformation occurs when information is applied. That's why each chapter first provides an explanation of the topic, followed by actionable steps to apply the information and facilitate a positive transformation in your mindset.

Throughout the book, you will be encouraged to consistently apply, practice, and benefit from your newfound knowledge, resulting in measurable growth with each step. Towards the end of the book, you will discover the "10-Day Positive Mindset Transformation," which serves as a how-to guide for applying your learnings daily and forming new positive habits.

You can explore subjects like gratitude, self-love, priming techniques, and basic meditation practices. You can also focus on daily affirmations, mastering the Law of Attraction, or gaining insights into synchronicities and vibrational energies. This intentional structure caters to your unique journey and individual needs.

Utilizing these tools will reclaim your power and unlock the path to experiencing happiness and joy, painting a life filled with abundance. These tools will empower you to achieve a state of graceful detachment when necessary, allowing you to stand firmly in your truth and navigate any challenge with an authentic smile. This comprehensive toolkit empowers you to realize your goals and desires and helps you sustain the ongoing happiness and joy that accompany them.

This approach adopts a holistic perspective, recognizing that practicing gratitude or visualizing goals alone isn't sufficient. It underscores the importance of alignment and maintaining a high-energy frequency. Utilizing all available tools can sustain positive momentum for lasting transformation. With a positive mindset as your foundation, you can manifest your dreams and discover profound happiness and fulfillment that truly sparks your spirit. However, this approach demands consistent effort. You must use these tools daily and integrate them into your life. It's not a one-time workshop but a lifelong journey of growth and transformation.

With this book, you have the ultimate power to master your thoughts and emotions. You can shape your life as you desire, taking complete control of your destiny. Understand and embrace that you can consciously choose to embrace positive or negative thoughts each day. It's a choice! Though this truth may seem deceptively simple, it's a profound realization that empowers you to create the life you genuinely want.

Pursuing a fulfilled and joyful life is an ongoing journey of continuous learning and growth. I actively engage in personal development by working with a life coach, reading weekly books, listening to podcasts, watching YouTube videos, and attending live events on various topics. I never cease my quest for knowledge and personal evolution. This journey brings me immense joy, especially when I see the transformative impact of my coaching on others. It's a true blessing to make a positive difference, spreading happiness and joy and providing the simple answers and tools I once sought. Yes, it truly is that simple.

Today is a fortunate day for you! I've condensed all my years of teaching and knowledge into this user-friendly book. It's designed to be simple and straightforward, making it easy for you to access and apply these teachings. Take full advantage of this valuable resource and tap into its wisdom. If a specific topic strikes a chord with you and you want to dive deeper, check out the recommended readings at the end of the book. Dive into your chosen subject to expand your knowledge and understanding.

Enjoy the journey and have fun exploring the vast possibilities that lie ahead.

And don't forget: It's all connected.

MANIFESTING IN ELEMENTARY SCHOOL

When I was in second grade, my best friend and I had a deep fascination with Fishertechnik toys. These toys were all about construction and taught us about simple machines, motorization, and mechanisms. Unfortunately, they were quite expensive, so the only time we could hope to get them was as Christmas gifts or for our birthdays.

We had our hearts set on the newest crane set and would often go window shopping at our favorite toy store after school. Waiting until Christmas seemed like an eternity, and it was disheartening to realize that our parents weren't planning to buy it for us. Despite this, we couldn't help but constantly talk about our dream toy.

One day, my best friend and I decided to take a stroll to our beloved playground, nestled in the heart of town and enclosed by a tall wooden fence and lush bushes. As we made our way to the backside of the playground, an extraordinary sight unfolded before our eyes. Each and every bush seemed to be decorated with either $10 or $20 bills. It was an unbelievable sight. Without a moment's hesitation, we dashed towards the bushes, eagerly gathering the unexpected treasure. It felt like a thrilling Easter egg hunt but with money as the prize. Once we had collected all the bills, we hurried back to Cliff's house, bursting with excitement, to proudly present our newfound wealth to Cliffs's mother.

To our amazement, the total amount we collected amounted to $1600. Our minds raced with excitement as we envisioned all the Fishertechnik toys we could purchase with such a substantial sum. However, our enthusiasm was short-lived when Cliff's mother intervened and firmly declared that we were not allowed to keep the money. In fact, she went a step further and promptly contacted the police. It seemed that she had doubts about our story, finding it hard to believe that the bushes were adorned with money.

The police informed us that a burglary at a nearby bike shop had occurred right before we arrived at the playground. Apparently, the thief had managed to snatch all the money from the cash register before making a hasty escape. However, the store clerk was not one to be easily deterred and gave chase. In his haste, the thief found himself burdened by the weight of the stolen cash and attempted to hide the money by tossing it over the fence of the playground. It was precisely at that moment that Cliff and I innocently stumbled upon the scene, unaware of the unfolding events.

Although the thief managed to evade capture, the bicycle shop owner was overjoyed that the stolen money had been recovered. In a gesture of gratitude, he generously rewarded both my friend and me with a 10% finder's fee, which was an enormous sum for two eight-year-olds. But the surprises didn't end there. In addition to the finder's fee, the shop owner presented us with a special gift as a token of appreciation for our honesty. To our sheer delight, it was none other than the coveted Fisher Technic Crane set we had dreamt of owning.

PART ONE
TRANSFORMING YOUR MINDSET

"JOURNALING
 IS A VOYAGE
 TO THE INTERIOR."

CHRISTINA BALDWIN

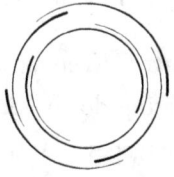

CHAPTER 1

YOUR JOURNAL

During this journey, having a journal is a necessity. Your journal acts as your sanctuary, allowing you to preserve your thoughts, experiences, ideas, and emotions. It's a very powerful tool for your transformation. Imagine it as your trusty sidekick while you read this book. It's not just a diary; it's your ticket to transforming your life and gaining crystal-clear insight into your desires and where you stand.

Think of your journal as the secret sauce for nailing your goals and gearing up for manifestation and visualization. It'll be your loyal companion as we uncover and conquer those pesky limiting beliefs that might hold you back from your dreams.

Whenever you need a hand in problem-solving or a dose of emotional well-being, your journal's got your back. It's like that dependable friend who's always there to listen, support, and help you be the best version of yourself. So, don't hold back!

And remember, you're in great company when you journal. Some of history's brightest minds, like Leonardo Da Vinci, Frida Kahlo, and Anne Frank, used journals as their canvas for self-reflection, creativity, and personal growth. You're joining a remarkable tradition of self-discovery and empowerment!

Here are a few reasons why journaling is beneficial in this process:

- **Memory-Boosting-Power:** Keeping a journal can provide memory-boosting power. Writing down your thoughts, experiences, and reflections in a journal engages your brain in a cognitive process that enhances memory retention. It's all thanks to two nifty cognitive tricks called the "generation effect" and the "encoding hypothesis." When you write things down, you actively engage with the material, processing and storing it in your memory. This active involvement can enhance your memory retention by up to 40%, compared to passive reading or listening. That's why journaling is a must-have tool on your path to personal transformation.

- **Clarity and Focus:** Writing down your desires, dreams, and goals helps clarify your thoughts. It allows you to articulate your wishes clearly and concisely, helping you better understand what you truly want to manifest. Journaling also helps you stay focused on your intentions, keeping them at the forefront of your mind.

- **Visualization Reinforcement:** By journaling about your desires, you reinforce the process of visualization. As you write, you can vividly imagine and describe the details of your desired outcome. This strengthens the neural pathways associated with your goals, making them more tangible and real in your mind.

- **Emotional Release and Alignment:** Journaling provides a safe space to express your emotions and release any doubts, fears, or limiting beliefs hindering your manifestation process. By acknowledging and addressing these emotions, you can work towards aligning your thoughts and beliefs with your desired outcome.

- **Tracking Progress and Celebrating Wins:** Keeping a journal allows you to track your progress along your manifestation journey. You can document any signs, synchronicities, or small wins that occur along the way. This serves as a reminder of your progress and boosts your confidence and motivation to continue manifesting.

- **Reflection and Self-Discovery:** Journaling provides an opportunity for self-reflection and self-discovery. As you write, you may uncover deeper insights, patterns, or limiting beliefs you previously knew about. This self-awareness is crucial for personal growth and allows you to make necessary adjustments to align your thoughts and actions with your desired manifestations.

Journaling is a personal journey, and there's no one-size-fits-all approach. Discover a journaling style that speaks to you, whether crafting affirmations, scripting your dreams, or simply pouring out your thoughts and feelings.

SUMMARY

Discover the power of journaling as a transformative tool. It clarifies desires, reinforces visualization, releases emotions, tracks progress, and encourages self-reflection. Due to the memory-boosting ability, you can retain the information you have learned much easier. Join a tradition of self-discovery and empowerment with your journal as a trusted companion on your journey.

"THE UNIVERSE IS NOT
SEPARATE FROM YOU;
IT IS EXPRESSING ITSELF
THROUGH YOU AT THIS
VERY MOMENT."

DEEPAK CHOPRA

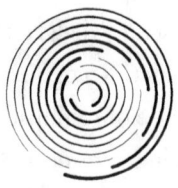

CHAPTER 2

INTERCONNECTEDNESS

As you reflect on interconnectedness, you'll realize that everything in our vast Universe is linked in ways that may be beyond complete understanding. It is the concept that everything in the world is interconnected and interdependent. This profound principle of interconnectedness means that you, as an individual, are an integral part of a grand network of connections and relationships, where every action, thought, and bit of energy has a profound impact, creating ripples through the interconnected web of existence.

Understanding interconnectedness is fundamental to your personal growth and spiritual journey. It involves awareness of the deep connection between your body, mind, and soul, cultivating harmony within yourself. This harmony extends to influence not only your energy but also the energy of those around you.

When you maintain a positive mindset, you shift your energy and contribute to a positive change in your environment and the world at large. As you find ease and embrace positivity, fulfillment, and happiness, you'll realize that it is all intricately connected. Every thought you think, every action you take, and every intention you set forth ripples through your life and beyond. It's a beautiful dance of interconnectedness, where everything you do affects you and resonates with the world around you.

Feeling interconnected is a beautiful experience that provides a sense of unity and understanding. It acknowledges that your well-being is linked with that of others and the planet. Recognizing and honoring this interconnectedness creates a greater sense of responsibility, harmony, and collective consciousness. You are intricately connected to others, and your actions and energy hold immense power, not only for yourself but also for others and the world. It's a gentle reminder that how you treat others reflects how you treat yourself.

The choices you make, the kindness you show, and the energy you give off have a powerful impact that spreads through the interconnected web of life. This profound truth calls you to embrace empathy, compassion, and the understanding that we are all in this together.

When you consider interconnectedness through the lens of karma, you understand that your actions, choices, and energy come back to you in some form. This awareness allows you to be more responsible for your actions, knowing they have consequences that extend beyond yourself and your immediate experiences. When you nurture a positive mindset, you attract positivity into your life and radiate it outwards, uplifting those around you.

Your thoughts, beliefs, and intentions shape your reality. When you align your desires with the well-being of others and the greater good, you tap into the interconnected nature of the Universe. This is vital for your dreams of happiness and fulfillment. As you dream big, you tap into the limitless potential that resides within you. Your dreams are not isolated fragments but interconnected visions that intertwine with the dreams of others. By embracing your dreams and pursuing them passionately, you contribute to the collective tapestry of aspirations, inspiring others to do the same.

By consistently directing your attention towards positive intentions and visualizing abundance and harmony for yourself and others, you attract experiences and opportunities that align with this interconnected vision. This is made possible through the Law of Attraction, as like attracts like.

As you wholeheartedly embrace the interconnectedness of all things, you have the power to cultivate unity, compassion, and responsibility, creating a harmonious and deeply connected world. Throughout your journey in life, may you create a tapestry of positivity, love, and fulfillment. It is important to remember that every thought, every action, and every dream you have is intricately linked to the grand symphony of existence, shaping your life and the world you inhabit.

ACTION ITEMS:

Embrace interconnectedness and start your journey toward positivity, love, and fulfillment here.

- **Practice Mindfulness:** Regularly engage in mindfulness exercises to become more aware of the present moment and your connection with all beings. This will help you recognize how your thoughts, emotions, and actions impact yourself and others.

- **Promote Positive Energy:** Cultivate a positive mindset and maintain a positive attitude to radiate positivity and uplift those around you. Remember that your energy has a powerful impact on the interconnected web of life.

- **Practice Empathy and Compassion:** Make a conscious effort to treat others with empathy and compassion, understanding that how you treat others reflects how you treat yourself. Recognize that we are all in this together.

- **Nurture Gratitude:** Embrace gratitude to acknowledge and appreciate the interconnected flow of blessings and experiences in your life. Shifting your perspective from scarcity to abundance helps deepen your sense of interconnectedness with the Universe.

- **Align Intentions with the Greater Good:** When setting intentions, align them with the well-being of others and the greater good. Recognize that your dreams and aspirations are interconnected with those of others, and by pursuing your goals with passion; you inspire others to do the same.

- **Practice the Law of Attraction:** Understand the power of manifesting and the Law of Attraction. Align your thoughts, emotions, and beliefs with your desires, tapping into the interconnected flow of the Universe to shape your reality.

- **Recognize the Impact of Choices:** Be aware that your actions, choices, and energy have consequences beyond yourself and your immediate experiences. Strive to make responsible choices that contribute positively to the interconnected web of life.

- **Embrace Unity and Responsibility:** Recognize the interconnected nature of all things and cultivate a sense of unity, responsibility, and collective consciousness. Understand that your well-being is linked with that of others and the planet.

- **Acknowledge Synchronicities:** Pay attention to synchronicities and meaningful coincidences in your life. They reveal a greater intelligence at play and invite trust in the interconnected nature of the Universe.

- **Inspire Positive Change:** As you become more aware of your interconnectedness, inspire positive change in your environment and the world. Encourage harmony, compassion, and responsibility in your interactions and actions.

- **Promote Harmony Within:** Understand the deep connection between your body, mind, and soul. Cultivate harmony within yourself, as it extends to influence not only your energy but also the energy of those around you.

- **Contribute to Collective Aspirations:** Recognize that your dreams are interconnected with the dreams of others. By passionately pursuing your dreams, you contribute to a collective tapestry of aspirations, inspiring others to follow their dreams.

SUMMARY

In your exploration of interconnectedness, you'll discover that everything in the vast Universe is profoundly linked. This principle of interconnectedness emphasizes that you are an integral part of a network of connections, where every action, thought, and bit of energy has a significant impact, creating ripples through existence. Recognizing this interconnectedness allows you to cultivate harmony, positivity, and responsibility within yourself, influencing your own life and the world around you. It's a reminder that you are part of a grand, interconnected web of existence, where your choices and energy hold immense power to shape your life and contribute to a harmonious, connected world.

"THE GREATEST DISCOVERY
OF ALL TIME IS THAT A
PERSON CAN CHANGE
THEIR FUTURE BY
MERELY CHANGING
THEIR ATTITUDE."

OPRAH WINFREY

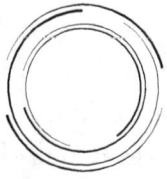

CHAPTER 3

A POSITIVE MINDSET

Establishing a positive mindset as the foundation of your life is paramount for numerous compelling reasons. Firstly, it brings you happiness and a deep sense of fulfillment. When you maintain a positive mindset, you approach life with optimism, gratitude, and resilience, allowing you to navigate challenges gracefully and find joy in even the smallest moments. It shapes your world perception, enabling you to focus on the positives and attract more positivity into your life.

Additionally, cultivating a positive mindset grants you a kind of superpower. When you vibrate on the energetic frequency of love, relaxation, and positivity, you tap into a state of alignment and flow. This alignment opens the doors to realizing your dreams and living a life of abundance. Maintaining a positive mindset makes you more receptive to opportunities, synchronicities, and possibilities that align with your desires.

Just like a house built on a solid foundation, having a positive mindset is the sturdy base upon which you can construct a fulfilling life. It provides stability, strength, and resilience, allowing you to weather the storms and enjoy the journey. Rather than feeling overwhelmed by setbacks, you view them as chances for personal development and education. Without a solid foundation, life can feel unstable and uncertain, making it difficult to manifest your dreams and sustain a sense of fulfillment. With a positive mindset, you are empowered to rebound with greater strength, discover innovative solutions, and persist in the face of adversity. It bolsters your belief in your capabilities and enhances your confidence to tackle new endeavors. With this newfound superpower, you grant yourself permission to dream big and set audacious goals.

Having a positive mindset is like having your very own magic wand for life! Imagine this: you wake up in the morning, and instead of grumbling about the day ahead, you greet it with a smile. That's the magic of a positive mindset. It's like having a superhero cape you can put on anytime. When life throws challenges at you, you don't just face them; you conquer them. You see opportunities in every problem, and you're unstoppable. You're saying, "Bring it on, world!"

But it's not just about conquering challenges; it's also about savoring the sweet moments. A positive mindset is like having a treasure map to happiness. You find joy in the simplest things, like a beautiful sunset, warm coffee, or a hug from a friend.

And here's the best part - it's contagious! When you radiate positivity, you lift others. You become a beacon of hope and inspiration. People are drawn to your optimism like moths to a flame. Your positivity becomes a force for good in the world.

You have the remarkable ability to transform your life through the uplifting force of a positive mindset. Make a choice to embrace this empowering shift daily and witness the incredible impact it can have on every aspect of your existence.

As you progress through the forthcoming chapters of this book, you will uncover an array of tools to incorporate into your daily routine, uplifting your energy and catalyzing a transformation in your mindset. Take a moment to peruse the summaries of the chapters that follow, and let the anticipation build for the exhilarating journey ahead.

While it may sound cliché, embarking on this adventure and engaging in the exercises is essential, and it's important to note that this is not a quick fix. Consistent daily effort is required, as consistency is the key to achieving success in this journey.

- **Gratitude:** Explore the transformative power of gratitude, shifting perspectives from scarcity to abundance and fostering a positive mindset. Embracing gratitude regularly enhances well-being, resilience, relationships, and happiness.
- **Priming:** This is a powerful psychological technique that unlocks the potential of your mind to embrace happiness and positivity. This transformative tool refreshes your mind and body, cultivating joy, relaxation, gratitude, and vivid visions of your future.
- **The "Happy State":** Changing your energetic state to a "Happy State" refers to intentionally transitioning to a joyful and fulfilling emotional or physical condition. This involves adjusting your physiology, focus, and language. Cultivating this skill enhances resilience, productivity, and limitless happiness. Being in a "Happy State" amplifies your manifestation power.
- **Mindfulness:** This practice involves being fully present and non-judgmentally aware of the current moment. This practice cultivates inner peace, emotional balance, and heightened awareness.
- **Mediation:** Engaging in meditation is a practice that can bring serenity and clarity to your mind, body, and spirit. It is a potent tool that aids in manifesting your desires and elevating your overall well-being by directing your focus toward positive thoughts and intentions.
- **"Love Yourself First":** The concept of "Love Yourself First" emphasizes the vital role of self-care in fostering personal well-being and nurturing healthy relationships. It involves acknowledging your inherent worth, embracing strengths and weaknesses, and tending to your physical, mental, and emotional needs.
- **The Happy Power Hour:** This is an intentional morning routine crafted to nurture personal growth and cultivate a positive mindset. While it may involve modifying your morning habits, its influence

on your day is profound. This self-care ritual encompasses practices like journaling, meditation, exercise, and reading.

- **Nourish and Move:** In today's fast-paced world, prioritizing well-being entails acknowledging the deep connection between healthy eating, physical activity, a positive mindset, and self-love. By nourishing your body with nutritious food and engaging in regular exercise, you reap physical health benefits and enhance cognitive function and mental clarity.

- **Your Peers:** Cultivating a supportive peer network is crucial for personal and professional growth. Surrounding yourself with individuals who challenge and uplift you brings diverse perspectives, fosters ongoing learning, provides accountability and support, contributes to personal development, and opens doors to valuable networking opportunities.

> Changing your mindset is a choice.
>
> Being happy is a choice.
>
> And to stay happy is a commitment!
>
> Happiness is not just a fleeting emotion;
>
> It is a conscious decision and a lifelong journey.

ACTION ITEMS:

As you delve into the upcoming chapters of this book and explore the tools provided, consider incorporating the following items to cultivate a positive mindset further. Embrace these actions and witness their transformative power, enabling you to navigate life with optimism and resilience.

- **Start your day with gratitude:** Begin each morning by expressing gratitude for the blessings in your life. Write down ten things you're grateful for to set a positive tone for the day.
- **Challenge negative thoughts:** Become aware of negative thoughts and actively challenge them. Replace them with positive affirmations or counter them with evidence that proves them wrong.
- **Leave the past in the past:** Don't waste your energy dwelling on painful or disheartening memories from your past. Remember, the past is behind you, and revisiting it will only bring more discomfort into the present. Instead, focus on cherishing the good memories and make a conscious decision to let go of the unpleasant ones.
- **Surround yourself with positivity:** Surround yourself with positive influences. Seek out uplifting books, podcasts, TV shows, and people who inspire and motivate you.
- **Practice self-care:** Prioritize self-care activities that nourish your mind, body, and soul. Engage in activities that bring you joy, such as exercise, meditation, or hobbies.
- **Focus on solutions, not problems:** Instead of dwelling on problems, focus on finding solutions. Train your mind to see challenges as opportunities for growth and learning.
- **Practice mindfulness:** Be present in the moment and cultivate mindfulness. Pay attention to your thoughts, feelings, and sensations without judgment. This helps you stay grounded and focused on the positive aspects of life.
- **Surround yourself with positive peers:** Surround yourself with supportive and positive individuals who uplift and encourage you. Limit your exposure to negative influences that drain your energy.
- **Celebrate small victories:** Acknowledge and celebrate your achievements, no matter how small. Recognize your progress and give yourself credit for your efforts.
- **Practice positive self-talk:** Replace self-criticism with positive self-

talk. Encourage and affirm yourself regularly. Remind yourself of your strengths and capabilities.

- **Embrace a growth mindset:** Adopt a growth mindset, believing you can learn, grow, and improve. Embrace challenges as opportunities for personal development and see failures as stepping stones to success.
- **Practice empathy and kindness:** Show empathy, kindness, and understanding towards others, which will create a positive ripple effect in your relationships and interactions.
- **Embrace resilience:** Rise above challenges and setbacks, refusing to let them define you. View obstacles as stepping stones on your path, knowing that they are temporary and you possess the strength and determination to conquer them.
- **End your day with gratitude:** End each day by expressing gratitude for the blessings you have encountered during the day. Write down ten things you're grateful for to set a positive tone for the next day. As you prepare to drift into sleep, make sure the final thought in your mind is a gratitude affirmation.

SUMMARY

A positive mindset is a superpower for conquering life's challenges and finding joy in simple moments. It's contagious, lifting others and fostering resilience. This mindset brings numerous benefits, empowering you to tackle setbacks, improve well-being, and most of all, it will support you to live a life in abundance. Embrace it for a vibrant, fulfilling life and positively impact the world.

"THE MORE GRATEFUL
I AM, THE MORE
BEAUTY I SEE."

MARY DAVIS

CHAPTER 4

GRATITUDE

For several reasons, gratitude is often considered one of the most powerful and transformative emotions. Gratitude shifts your perspective from what you lack to what you have. It encourages you to focus on the positives in your life, no matter how small they may seem. This positive perspective can significantly improve your well-being and the world around you. Your daily gratitude practice serves as the cornerstone of your positive mindset. By consistently engaging in gratitude, you lay a solid foundation for cultivating a mindset focused on your life's positives. Most importantly, developing a grateful mindset changes your energetic vibration to a positive frequency and attracts more good things into your life.

Gratitude is a concept found in various religious and philosophical traditions, including Buddhism, Christianity, Islam, and many ancient religions. Overall, these religious and philosophical traditions emphasize the significance of gratitude as a means of acknowledging blessings, fostering humility, and nurturing a sense of contentment and inner peace. Gratitude is often seen as a virtue that can lead to spiritual growth and a deeper connection with the divine.

Cultivating a mindset of gratitude is essential for personal growth and happiness. When you practice gratitude, you recognize and appreciate the blessings, experiences, and people that bring you joy and fulfillment and elevate your energetic vibration to the highest level. Gratitude isn't just an emotion; it's a powerful tool that can shape your mindset and transform your life. By consistently focusing on the positives in your life, you train your mind to seek out and amplify the good.

Gratitude is a skill that can be honed over time. The more you practice it, the more natural it becomes to find reasons to be grateful. It's like exercising a muscle - the more you work on it, the stronger it becomes. By actively cultivating gratitude, you strengthen your ability to shift your perspective and embrace a mindset of abundance and positivity. Remember, your energetic vibration is crucial in manifesting your dreams and desires. When you approach life with gratitude, you raise your energetic frequency and align yourself with the highest level of positivity and possibility. This elevated vibration attracts more opportunities, synchronicities, and blessings into your life. So, take charge of your mindset and embrace the power of gratitude. Cultivate a daily practice of acknowledging and appreciating the positives in your life.

ACTION ITEMS:

Take out your journal and get busy writing down what you are grateful for. By documenting your gratitude, you create a tangible record of your life's blessings and positive experiences. Your gratitude journal allows you to delve deeper into the emotions associated with gratitude, and it will help you cultivate a greater sense of mindfulness and awareness of the abundance surrounding you.

- **Simple Gratitude:** The simplest technique is to start your day by taking a moment to ponder and write down ten things that fill you with gratitude. They can be as simple and beautiful as the morning sunshine, the warmth of your family, the comfort of your home, or the taste of a delicious meal. You can be grateful for your health, job, or last vacation.

- **Gratitude for Accomplishments:** Taking your gratitude practice to the next level involves appreciating what you currently have and acknowledging and being grateful for the accomplishments and moments that have brought you pride in your life. Reflecting on your achievements, big or small, can evoke a sense of gratitude and fulfillment. Recognize the hard work, dedication, and growth that led you to those accomplishments.

- **Gratitude for Family and Friends:** Being grateful for the moments of happiness shared with family and friends is a beautiful way to deepen your gratitude practice. Recall those joyful times when you were all together, laughing and creating cherished memories. These moments of connection and love are precious, and expressing gratitude strengthens your bonds and brings more positivity into your relationships.

- **Gratitude for Funny Moments:** Recall funny moments that made you laugh wholeheartedly. Laughter is a powerful source of joy and can instantly uplift your spirits. Be grateful for those moments of pure laughter and the lightness they brought to your life.

- **Gratitude for Romantic and Sexy Moments**: Go back in time and find those moments that made your heart flutter or filled you with deep love. They can evoke a profound sense of gratitude. These moments of connection and vulnerability are worth cherishing, and expressing gratitude for them allows you to relive and appreciate the beauty of those experiences.

- **Gratitude for Exciting Moments:** Feeling gratitude for exciting moments means recognizing and appreciating the exhilarating experiences that have brought you joy, enthusiasm, and a sense of adventure. These moments could be when you step out of your comfort zone, achieve something remarkable, or feel excitement and anticipation.

- **Future Gratitude:** Now take your gratitude to the next level by projecting your attitude of gratefulness into the future. Be grateful for the **Future Accomplishments** you aspire to achieve, the happiness you will share with your **Family and Friends**, the **Funny Moments** that will make you laugh, the **Romantic Moments** that will fill your heart with love, and the **Exciting Moments** to come that ignite your passion.

- By expressing gratitude for these future moments, you set a positive intention and align your energy toward manifesting those goals. This practice keeps you motivated and opens up opportunities and possibilities for growth and success. Gratitude is a powerful tool to strengthen your visualization process because it creates joy and positivity.

- **Variety Matters:** Try not to write down and repeat the same things every day. Look for new aspects of your life to be grateful for. This keeps the practice fresh and prevents it from becoming routine.

- **Harness the power of gratitude as an affirmation:** Take the things you're thankful for and reaffirm them throughout your day. Whether you're working out, walking your dog, or handling household chores like dishes or laundry, repeat these gratitude affirmations. Through repetition, this potent emotion truly embeds itself into your being.

- **Gratitude meditation:** During meditation, focus on the sensations of gratitude in your body and allow yourself to experience the positive emotions associated with them entirely. You can also mentally express gratitude towards yourself, others, and the Universe. Don't just go through the motions; genuinely feel the gratitude in your heart. This emotional connection makes the practice more powerful.

- **Expressing gratitude to others:** Take time to thank the people in your life who have made a difference. Showing appreciation to others not only benefits them but also reinforces your sense of gratitude. Write a heartfelt thank-you note, have a conversation expressing your appreciation, or perform acts of kindness to show your gratitude. Sharing your gratitude not only benefits others but also strengthens your sense of connection and positivity.

- **Engage in a Gratitude Reflection Ritual:** Before drifting into a peaceful sleep, take a moment to revisit the positive experiences and moments of gratitude that filled your day. This simple practice allows you to cherish the goodness that unfolded and redirects your attention away from negativity or obstacles. By making gratitude your final thought of the day, you send this powerful emotion to your subconscious. Cultivate the habit of concluding your day with a heartfelt "thank you."
- **Gratitude in challenging times:** Even during difficult times, there are often silver linings or lessons to be learned. Practice finding gratitude amid challenges by focusing on personal growth, resilience, or the support you receive from others.

Regularly practicing gratitude will shift your perspective towards a more positive and appreciative mindset. It will enhance your overall well-being, increase resilience, improve relationships, and foster a greater sense of happiness.

Gratitude is a personal practice, and finding what works best for you is essential. Experiment with different gratitude practices and find the ones that most resonate with you.

SUMMARY

Delve into the profound impact of gratitude, highlighting its transformative ability to shift perspectives from scarcity to abundance and cultivate a positive mindset. Rooted in diverse spiritual and philosophical traditions, gratitude is revered as a virtue that fosters inner peace and spiritual growth. Regularly embracing gratitude will enhance well-being, resilience, relationships, and happiness.

"EMPOWERMENT IS ABOUT
TAKING OWNERSHIP OF
YOUR LIFE, EMBRACING
YOUR STRENGTHS, AND
USING THEM TO CREATE
THE LIFE YOU DESIRE."

TONY ROBBINS

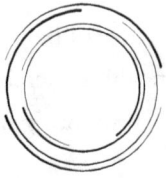

CHAPTER 5

PRIMING

Tap into the power of priming and unlock the secrets of your mind. This incredible technique is a psychological powerhouse that paves the way for your mind to embrace pure happiness. It's a game-changer that allows you to refresh your mind and body, cultivating feelings of joy, relaxation, gratitude, and vibrant visions of your future. This remarkable tool acts as a guiding light, aligning your emotions and thoughts with a positive mindset. Best of all, it seamlessly fits into your daily routine, whether it's the golden moments of the morning, the tranquil hours before sleep, or whenever it suits you best.

ACTION ITEMS:

Whether you're seeking a quick pick-me-up or incorporating this technique into your daily routine, it will positively impact your body's chemical composition and promote happiness. Before diving in, take a moment to review your gratitude list in your journal. Find a comfortable seat and prepare to engage in a practice that combines Bellows Breath, gratitude, and visualization.

Step 1: Bellows Breath

Begin with the invigorating practice of Bellows Breath, also known as Bhastrika Pranayama. This yogic breathing exercise involves rhythmic and forceful inhalations and exhalations, promoting physical and mental well-being.

- **Sit Comfortably**: Find a comfortable position in a chair with your back straight.
- **Relax**: Close your eyes and take a few deep, calming breaths to relax your body and mind.
- **Begin the Breath**: Inhale forcefully and deeply through your nostrils, filling your lungs thoroughly. This inhalation should be swift and potent, akin to a confident "sniff."
- **Exhale with Force**: Exhale vigorously and entirely through your nostrils, expelling the air rapidly. This exhalation should also be brisk, resembling a determined "sniff out." (Keep a tissue handy) If you feel comfortable you might try raising your arms above your head during inhalation and bringing them down rapidly during exhalation.
- **Rhythm**: Maintain this rhythmic pattern of forceful inhalations and exhalations for 3 sets, with 30 breath counts in each set. One inhale and one exhale constitute 1 count. The breaths should have equal durations, creating a steady and continuous flow.
- **Keep It Comfortable**: Begin slowly and gently, gradually increasing the speed as you become more accustomed to the technique. Avoid straining or overexerting yourself.
- **Duration**: Practice the Bellows Breath for approximately 1-2 minutes.
- **Rest**: After completing this breathing technique, take a few normal breaths to return to a state of calm.

Step 2: Gratitude and Visualization

- **Gratitude:** While seated with your eyes closed, place your hands on your heart. Reflect on three instances in your life when you felt profound gratitude.
- **Pride and Accomplishments**: With your eyes still closed, think of three moments in your life when you felt a deep sense of pride or a sense of accomplishment.
- **Happiness**: Continue seated, eyes closed, and bring to mind three instances when you experienced genuine happiness or shared heartfelt laughter.
- **Future Gratitude:** As you maintain your seated position with closed eyes, envision three future moments in your life that you will be grateful for once your dreams and desires have become reality. Visualize your goals as if they have already manifested. Immerse yourself in the emotions and elation associated with these achievements. Wear a smile and openly express gratitude for each upcoming moment that you will treasure.

> **SUMMARY**
> Priming is a powerful psychological technique that allows you to tap into the potential of your mind to embrace happiness and positivity. It's a transformative tool that will help you refresh your mind and body, fostering feelings of joy, relaxation, gratitude, and vivid visions of your future.

"YOU ARE THE ONLY ONE WHO CAN EMPOWER YOURSELF. NO ONE ELSE CAN DO IT FOR YOU."

LES BROWN

CHAPTER 6

THE HAPPY STATE

The art of "changing your state" is a profound journey towards intentionally shifting your emotional or physical condition into a more desirable one—a "Happy State." It's about becoming fully conscious and purposefully adjusting your thoughts, emotions, or physical sensations to craft a state of being that's not just positive but profoundly joyful and fulfilling.

Empower yourself by shifting your state when you notice your energy waning, when feelings of exhaustion, overwhelm, or negativity start to take over your thoughts. The three key elements that you can influence instantly are your physiology, your focus, and the language you use.

1. **Physiology:** This is how you use your body, including your posture, breathing, and movement. Your physical state has a significant impact on your emotions and your overall well-being. You will positively influence your mental and emotional state by consciously adjusting your physiology, such as standing tall, taking deep breaths, or engaging in physical activity.

   Two Minute Power Pose: In just two minutes, you will transform your body chemistry by making a simple adjustment to your physical state. Stand tall with your shoulders back, and lift your head high. Imagine your favorite superhero movie and strike a pose that embodies strength and confidence. Whenever you sense yourself falling into a slump, don't hesitate—assume your power pose for just two minutes and flash a smile. Standing in your pose, you'll feel the shift in your energy and mindset, empowering yourself to tackle whatever comes your way. It sounds silly, but it works wonders.

2. **Focus:** Energy flows where focus goes. Your focus directs your emotional energy. In simpler terms, what you choose to concentrate on in your thoughts generates feelings that significantly shape your life experiences and outcomes. Your mental and emotional energy will naturally follow where you place your attention.

    Consistently, what you focus on tends to manifest in your reality. When you wholeheartedly believe in and concentrate on achieving your goals, you're more inclined to take actions that propel you toward success. Conversely, if self-doubt and a fixation on failure dominate your thoughts, you're more likely to manifest those negative outcomes through self-fulfilling prophecies. So, make the powerful choice to center your focus on your "Happy State" and the ambitious goals you've set for your life.

3. **Language:** Language refers to the words you use to describe your experiences, both internally and externally. Be mindful because your chosen words shape your thoughts, emotions, and beliefs. When you use empowering and positive language, you can reframe your experiences and create a more empowering narrative. Uplifting self-talk is a powerful tool that can transform your inner dialogue. Instead of dwelling on limitations or negative aspects, you can focus on your strengths, achievements, and potential.

    Always remember, changing your state to a "Happy State" is a practice that calls for self-awareness, intention, and consistent dedication. As you nurture this skill, you'll fortify your resilience, supercharge your productivity, and ultimately bask in the radiant light of boundless happiness. Simply continue to wear that happy smile on your face.

When you explore the Law of Attraction and begin manifesting and visualizing your goals, make sure you're in your "Happy State." This is crucial because the power of manifestation is amplified when you operate from this joyful state of being. Your happiness elevates your energy to its highest frequency, and this elevated vibration accelerates the attraction of your desires.

ACTION ITEMS:

Here are some action items to complement your physiology, focus, and language changes – all designed to help you enter your "Happy State." Pick the ones that resonate with you the most. You hold the reins of your emotions and can steer your journey towards happiness with purpose and determination.

Gratitude Exercise:

Direct your attention towards the abundance of positive aspects in your life, both in the present moment and the future that awaits you.

Present Moment:

- Write down 10 things you are grateful for in the present moment.

Pride and Joy:

- List 10 things that make you feel proud, such as accomplishments or praise.
- Recall and jot down 10 instances when you had a hearty laugh. Feel

the joy and humor of these moments.

Future Moments:

- Craft 10 things you will be grateful for in the future because you know that all your dreams will come true, and you will feel happiness.

Smile Activation:

- Put on a smile, even if it feels forced, and maintain it for 2-5 minutes. Smiling activates the well-known happy hormones, creating a positive feedback loop in your body and mind. Releasing endorphins, serotonin, dopamine, and oxytocin will uplift your mood, reduce stress, and contribute to a sense of happiness and well-being.
- Watch a funny movie or video, and make yourself laugh.

Happy Music Playlist:

- Create a playlist filled with your favorite happy tunes. Have it readily available for when you need a mood boost.

Move Your Body

- **Dance Break:** Put on that happy music, and get up and dance! Just 3-5 minutes of crazy, joyous dancing can transform your body chemistry into a "Happy State". Keep on smiling while you dance. This technique is also helpful when you have worked on a single task for longer than 30 minutes. Shake it out and feel your energy and productivity rise again.
- **Power walk:** How about going for a power walk? Or go on a run? Slip on those sneakers, step out, and let the magic happen. When you briskly walk or run, something remarkable occurs – your body releases those delightful "feel-good" hormones. Endorphin, serotonin, dopamine, and norepinephrine. These little wonders have a

knack for turning your mood around, whisking you into a happier state. It's like a domino effect: when your body feels good, your mind often follows suit. As you stride, you can let out that pent-up tension and stress through your movements, almost like shaking it off. It's a fantastic way to release and manage stress more effectively. And guess what? You can make it even better by chanting positive incantations while walking. It's like a double boost for your body and mind.

Deep Breathing:

- Stand tall and inhale slowly through your nose, filling your belly with air. Exhale entirely through your mouth.
- This breathing technique activates your body's relaxation response, reducing stress, promoting calmness, and increasing oxygen flow. Focusing on your breath and taking deep, intentional breaths can quickly shift your state to a more relaxed and centered state of being.

Positive-Self-Talk:

Positive self-talk is a powerful practice that involves consciously using uplifting and encouraging language when speaking to yourself. It's a way to cultivate a positive mindset, boost self-confidence, and improve overall well-being. Here are some recommendations for incorporating positive self-talk into your daily life:

- **Awareness:** Start by becoming aware of your inner dialogue. Notice any negative or self-critical thoughts that arise throughout the day. Pay attention to the language you use when talking to yourself.
- **Reframe negative thoughts:** When you think negatively, consciously reframe those thoughts into positive and empowering statements. For example, if you think, "I can't do this," reframe it as "I can do it. I am capable and ready to handle this challenge."
- **Use affirmations:** Create positive affirmations that resonate with you and reflect the qualities or beliefs you want to embody. Repeat

these affirmations to yourself regularly, especially during self-doubt or difficulty. For example, say, "I am worthy of love and success" or "I have the power to overcome any obstacle."

- **Practice self-compassion:** Be kind and compassionate towards yourself, especially during struggles or setbacks. Treat yourself with the kindness and understanding you would offer a dear friend. Replace self-criticism with self-compassion and encouragement.

Congratulations! You've achieved remarkable self-awareness, recognizing those moments when your thoughts attempt to drag you down. Embrace this awareness as a powerful gift, empowering you to transition into a "Happy State."

SUMMARY

Changing your state to a 'Happy State'" is about intentionally shifting your emotional or physical condition to a joyful and fulfilling state. You can do this by adjusting your physiology, focus, and language. Practicing this skill leads to resilience, productivity, and boundless happiness. When working with the Law of Attraction, being in a "Happy State" amplifies your manifestation power.

"THE PURPOSE OF OUR LIVES IS TO BE HAPPY, AND MINDFULNESS IS THE KEY TO UNLOCKING THAT HAPPINESS."

DALAI LAMA

CHAPTER 7

MINDFULNESS

Think of mindfulness as an incredible superpower you can apply to your everyday life. It's a simple practice where you fully embrace the present moment without passing judgment on yourself or your surroundings. When you embrace mindfulness, you will discover contentment in the simple joys of life, ultimately leading to greater happiness.

The Dalai Lama, a highly respected spiritual leader, frequently emphasizes the profound significance of mindfulness in his various writings and teachings. He regards mindfulness as a valuable practice that can lead you towards inner tranquility, compassion, and a more profound understanding of yourself and others. By being mindful, you can become more aware of your thoughts, emotions, and reactions. This heightened awareness empowers you to manage negative emotions, fostering emotional balance and reducing suffering.

It's a powerful tool that taps into your inner strength, offering daily clarity, focus, and calmness. Through mindfulness, you'll experience a significant reduction in stress, an enhancement of your mental well-being, and an overall improvement in your quality of life. Mindfulness empowers you to infuse more peace, awareness, and joy into your life.

You'll unlock incredible potential within, leading to a life marked by balance, fulfillment, and a profound connection with the present moment. Mindfulness is your secret recipe for a more vibrant, focused, and serene life—a daily reminder that the real magic unfolds in the present.

ACTION ITEMS:

Mindfulness is a skill that flourishes with practice. Begin with small moments of mindfulness and gradually expand your practice. These empowering practices start with your journey to greater presence, self-awareness, and inner peace.

- **Mindful Breathing:** Take a few moments to connect with your breath. Feel each inhale and exhale, allowing yourself to be fully present in breathing.
- **Body Scan:** Conduct a gentle, head-to-toe scan of your body. Notice any sensations or areas of tension with kindness and curiosity.
- **Mindful Eating:** Elevate your mealtime experience by engaging all your senses. Savor each bite, exploring flavors, textures, and aromas mindfully.
- **Walking Meditation:** Turn your daily walk into a meditative practice. Focus on the sensation of your feet meeting the ground and the graceful movement of your body.
- **Mindful Listening:** Immerse yourself in the sounds around you, whether it's the beauty of nature, the melody of music, or the art of conversation. Be fully present, leaving judgments and distractions behind.
- **Gratitude Practice:** Take a moment to reflect on and celebrate the blessings in your life. Cultivate an attitude of appreciation for both the big and small things.
- **Mindful Journaling:** Create a safe space for your thoughts and emo-

tions. Write without judgment, allowing your inner world to flow freely onto the pages.

- **Mindful Self-Compassion:** Extend kindness to yourself. Acknowledge your struggles with understanding and offer yourself the gift of self-compassion.
- **Mindful Technology Use:** Carve out dedicated moments to disconnect from screens. Rediscover the beauty of the present moment, free from digital distractions.
- **Mindful Communication:** Elevate your interactions by being fully present in conversations. Practice active listening, offering your undivided attention to those you engage with.

SUMMARY

There is a transformative power called mindfulness. Mindfulness is being fully present and aware of the present moment without judgment. This practice fosters inner peace, emotional balance, and heightened awareness. The Dalai Lama underscores its significance, and through simple practices like mindful breathing, body scans, and gratitude, you can unlock its potential, leading to a more focused, serene, and fulfilling life.

"MEDITATION IS THE ART OF SILENCING THE MIND AND EXPERIENCING THE BLISS OF THE PRESENT MOMENT."

DEEPAK CHOPRA

CHAPTER 8

MEDITATION

Meditation is like a soothing balm for your mind, body, and spirit, bringing you tranquility and clarity. It is also a powerful tool for manifesting your desires and enhancing your well-being. By meditating and focusing on positive thoughts and intentions, you can more easily attract more of what you want into your life.

Contrary to the misconception that meditation involves forcing the mind to stop thinking, it is not about suppressing or controlling thoughts. Instead, meditation is a practice of cultivating awareness and observing the thoughts that arise without judgment. It is about creating a space of stillness and allowing thoughts to come and go naturally without getting entangled. Developing a non-reactive and non-judgmental relationship with your thoughts can cultivate a sense of inner calm, clarity, and presence. Meditation teaches you to observe your thoughts with curiosity and compassion, ultimately leading to a greater understanding of yourself and the nature of your mind.

With the various meditation techniques available to you, it will be easy to find one that you resonate with. Meditation is a simple and straightforward practice. Whatever practice you choose, you can start training your mind to focus and redirect your thoughts, ultimately leading to mental clarity, relaxation, and inner peace. Embrace the beauty of meditation as your unique journey, for there is no universal path to follow. It's a personal odyssey where you choose the techniques that resonate with your soul. Be patient with yourself, for this discovery may take time, but the journey is a profound teacher.

As a beginner, consider commencing with brief sessions, as short as 5 minutes, and then gradually extend your practice like a rising sun. In these precious moments of stillness, you'll hush the inner chatter, paving the way for the manifestation and visualization of your most cherished goals. Your path is your own, and with every mindful breath, you're creating a masterpiece of inner peace and empowerment.

Common meditation practices include:

- **Mindfulness meditation:** This involves focusing on your breath, bodily sensations, or your present-moment experiences without judgment. The aim is to observe your thoughts and emotions as they arise, allowing them to pass without getting caught up in them. Acknowledge and let them go.
- **Loving-kindness meditation:** In this practice, you cultivate feelings of love, compassion, and kindness towards yourself and others. You can silently repeat positive affirmations or visualize sending well-wishes to yourself and others.
- **Transcendental meditation:** With this technique, you use a mantra—a word, sound, or phrase—to help you focus your mind and achieve a state of deep relaxation and inner awareness.
- **Guided meditation:** In this meditation style, you follow along with a prerecorded or live guide who offers guidance and cues for relaxation, visualization, or introspection. You can discover a wide array of guided meditation sessions on platforms like YouTube and various mobile apps.

ACTION ITEMS:

Select the practice that truly speaks to your heart to calm your mind and fully immerse yourself in the present moment. Remember, the meditation techniques offered are just the tip of the iceberg. A world of diverse practices is waiting for you to explore, offering endless possibilities to enrich your inner journey with enthusiasm and joy.

1. **Mindfulness Meditation:**
   This mindfulness meditation is a powerful tool. It is perfect for a quick reset during a busy day or as a brief moment of relaxation and centering. It can help you become more aware of the present moment and reduce stress and mental clutter. You can extend the duration as you become more comfortable with the practice. Set a timer.

   - Find a quiet and comfortable place to sit or stand.
   - Close your eyes gently, or if you prefer, keep them softly focused on a spot in front of you.
   - Take a deep breath through your nose, allowing your lungs to fill with air.
   - As you exhale through your mouth, release any tension and let go of any worries or distractions.
   - Now, bring your attention to your breath. Notice the sensation of your breath entering and leaving your nostrils or the rise and fall of your chest or abdomen.
   - Stay fully present with each breath, observing the natural rhythm without trying to change it.
   - If your mind starts to wander or become aware of any thoughts, gently acknowledge them without judgment, then gently guide your focus back to your breath.
   - Continue this practice for a minute or two, staying attuned to your breath and the present moment.

- When you're ready, slowly open your eyes and take a moment to appreciate the calm and presence you've cultivated.

2. **Loving-Kindness Meditation:**

    This short loving-kindness meditation is a wonderful way to cultivate feelings of compassion and empathy for yourself and others in just a few minutes. You can adjust the phrases and the duration to fit your preferences and available time.

    Start with finding a comfortable and quiet place to sit or lie down. Close your eyes and take a few deep, relaxing breaths to center yourself. Begin by directing loving-kindness towards yourself. In your mind, repeat these phrases:

    - "May I be happy."
    - "May I be healthy."
    - "May I be safe."
    - "May I live with ease."

    After a few moments of focusing on yourself, shift your attention to someone you care about deeply, like a close friend or family member. Visualize them in your mind's eye, and repeat the same phrases for them:

    - "May you be happy."
    - "May you be healthy."
    - "May you be safe."
    - "May you live with ease."

    Now, extend your loving-kindness to all living beings:

    - "May all beings be happy."
    - "May all beings be healthy."
    - "May all beings be safe."

- "May all beings live with ease."

Sit quietly for a moment, continuing to send these well-wishes to yourself and others. When you're ready, open your eyes and carry this sense of loving-kindness and goodwill throughout your day.

3. **Transcendental Meditation:**

This transcendental meditation is a technique that involves silently repeating a specific mantra to achieve a deep state of restful awareness and reduce stress. Feel free to craft your incantations and recite them repeatedly, or you can select from these provided mantras:

"Peace": Repeating this word can help invoke a sense of inner calm.

"Stillness": This mantra can guide you to a serene and tranquil state of mind.

"Happiness": It encourages you to reflect on the things that bring you happiness and gratitude in your life, which can boost your overall well-being.

- Find a quiet and comfortable place to sit with your eyes closed.
- Begin by taking a few deep breaths to relax your body and settle your mind.
- Choose a mantra that resonates with you. It can be a simple word or sound.
- Silently repeat the mantra in your mind, allowing it to flow with each breath effortlessly.
- As thoughts or distractions arise, gently bring your attention back to the mantra, letting go of any attachment to the thoughts.
- Continue this process for about 10-20 minutes, allowing yourself to sink into deep relaxation and inner stillness.
- When the time is up, gradually bring your awareness back to

the present moment, gently opening your eyes and taking a few moments to reorient yourself.

4. **The 5-5-5 breathing technique- a power tool:**

This breathing technique is a valuable tool for cultivating mindfulness and managing stress. This technique involves regulating your breath by inhaling for a count of five, holding the breath for a count of five, and then exhaling for a count of five. This technique has immense power in soothing your nervous system.

Here's how it works:

- **Inhale (5 seconds)**: Take a slow, deep breath through your nose, counting to five as you fill your lungs with air. This slow inhalation helps calm your nervous system.
- **Hold (5 seconds)**: After you've inhaled, hold your breath for a count of five. This brief pause lets you focus on the present moment and the breath itself.
- **Exhale (5 seconds)**: Slowly release your breath through your mouth for a count of five. As you exhale, imagine letting go of any tension or stress.

To make the most of this breathing technique, it's essential to customize the counts to a comfortable and natural pace. If you're new to this practice, repeat the breathing pattern for a minimum of 10 counts. This simple yet effective technique can be easily integrated into your daily routine, serving as a powerful tool to cultivate mindfulness and effectively manage stress.

The 5-5-5 breathing technique serves several purposes:

- **Stress Reduction**: It helps reduce stress and anxiety by promoting relaxation and slowing down the racing thoughts often accompanying stressful situations.
- **Mindfulness**: The technique encourages mindfulness by di-

recting your attention to the breath and counting rhythm. It anchors you in the present moment.

- **Calming**: The even, controlled breath pattern soothes the nervous system, bringing a sense of calm and balance.
- **Preparation**: You can use this technique before challenging situations, such as public speaking or critical encounters, to center yourself and reduce anxiety.
- **Promoting Happiness**: By regulating your breath and calming the mind, the 5-5-5 breathing technique can contribute to a sense of inner peace and contentment, fostering a "happy state."

SUMMARY

Meditation is a transformative practice that brings tranquility and clarity to mind, body, and spirit. It is a powerful tool for manifesting your desires and enhancing overall well-being by focusing on positive thoughts and intentions. Meditation offers a variety of techniques, such as mindfulness, loving-kindness, transcendental, and guided meditation, making it accessible to everyone. The meditation journey is personal and evolves over time, allowing you to gradually extend your practice and harness the benefits of inner peace and empowerment.

"TO BE BEAUTIFUL MEANS
TO BE YOURSELF. YOU DON'T
NEED TO BE ACCEPTED BY OTHERS
YOU NEED TO ACCEPT YOURSELF."

THICH NHAT HANH

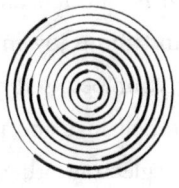

CHAPTER 9

LOVE YOURSELF FIRST

Self-love is about recognizing your worth, embracing your strengths and weaknesses, and caring for your physical, mental, and emotional needs. It's like discovering your inner sanctuary. It means prioritizing your well-being, happiness, and fulfillment. It involves treating yourself with kindness, compassion, and respect.

By "Loving Yourself First," you ensure that you are healthy enough to give and contribute to others. When you practice self-care, you can give love to others and receive it because you know you are worthy of being loved. Simply put, when you love yourself, you are in a better position to cultivate healthy relationships with others. You won't rely on external validation or expect others to fill emotional voids. Your self-love strengthens your emotional resilience, allowing you to handle setbacks and failures more gracefully because your self-worth isn't solely dependent on external achievements. You stand in your truth.

You will also discover that when you "Love Yourself First"; you develop a drive for personal development, self-improvement, and growth. You now possess the power and confidence to boldly pursue your goals, try new things, and take risks without feeling guilty. Love for oneself brings happiness, and self-love contributes to that happiness.

When you treat yourself with kindness and respect, you naturally experience greater contentment and more joy in your daily life. Overall, self-love empowers you to bring your best self to the table and significantly impact the world around you. Self-love and personal development are not about being self-centered or neglecting others; it's about finding a healthy balance that allows you to grow, thrive, and contribute to the well-being of yourself and those around you.

Being "Selfish"

Being a bit "selfish" regarding self-care is a positive thing. Being "selfish" means making self-care a non-negotiable part of your routine. It's about recognizing that you can't pour from an empty cup. Being "selfish" allows you to set boundaries and protect your time and energy. It's about saying "no" when necessary to avoid burnout. Both loving yourself first and being selfish sometimes empower you to take control of your life. By making decisions that align with your values and goals, you assert your autonomy and resist the pressure of others' expectations. When you stand firmly in your truth and believe in yourself, your impact on those around you becomes even more significant. Embrace the anticipation of a self-confidence boost and the profound sense of contentment and fulfillment accompanying it.

In essence, loving yourself first and embracing a degree of "selfishness" in personal development are about recognizing your value and taking steps to live a more fulfilling and authentic life. It's not about disregarding others or being egocentric but rather about creating a strong foundation for personal growth and positive relationships. When you prioritize self-love and self-care, you become better equipped to give back and contribute positively to the world around you.

ACTION ITEMS:

"Loving Yourself First" is an ongoing journey that will contribute to your positive mindset and karma. The process takes time, so be patient and gentle as you incorporate these action items into your life. Each step brings you closer to a more profound sense of self-love, fulfillment, and happiness. Take out your journal and begin your journey to your happy place.

- **Prioritize self-care:** Make a list of activities that bring you joy and make you feel nourished. Then, start implementing these activities into your daily life. Schedule regular self-care practices such as meditation, exercise, getting a massage, reading, spending time in nature, or meeting your best friends for coffee. Commit to making self-care a non-negotiable part of your routine.

- **Set healthy boundaries:** Identify areas in your life where you need to establish boundaries to protect your emotional well-being. Look closely at your relationships, children, partner, family, and friends. Learn to say "no" to things that drain your energy or compromise your values. Learn to stand in your power. It is ok to say "no". Surround yourself with people who support and uplift you.

- **Practice self-compassion:** Treat yourself with kindness and understanding. When faced with self-criticism or negative self-talk, challenge those thoughts and replace them with positive affirmations. Celebrate your achievements, no matter how small, and forgive yourself for any mistakes or setbacks. What if all your setbacks are set up for something bigger and better to come, only that you haven't seen yet? Treat yourself with the same kindness and understanding you would offer a friend, and replace self-criticism with self-compassion.

- **Engage in self-reflection:** Take time to reflect on your values, passions, and goals. Use your journal as your power tool for self-discovery and self-expression. Explore your strengths, interests, and desires, and align your actions with your authentic self.

- **Cultivate gratitude:** Develop a daily gratitude practice by acknowledging and appreciating the positive aspects of your life. Write down ten things you are grateful for, then focus on ten things that you love about yourself and that makes you feel proud and happy. This practice can shift your focus towards self-love and create a positive mindset.

Affirmations for self-love:

Incorporating positive affirmations into your daily routine will profoundly transform your mindset and overall well-being. Say these affirmations with intention and belief, allowing them to empower you and reinforce the practice of self-love. Embrace your worthiness and let the love within you radiate outwards.

- I am worthy of love and respect, and I prioritize my well-being.
- I care for myself daily, nurturing my mind, body, and soul.
- I accept and love my unique qualities and strengths.
- I set healthy boundaries to protect my emotional well-being.
- I deserve happiness and fulfillment, and I prioritize my joy and inner peace.

Incantations for self-love:

Incantations are most impactful when you say them over and over again. This repetition helps reinforce the belief or intention you express through the incantation, making it more deeply ingrained in your subconscious mind and ultimately more effective in influencing your thoughts and actions. The more you repeat these incantations, the more they can shape your mindset and help you manifest a positive relationship towards yourself. You are deserving of all the love and happiness in the world!

- "I am worthy of love and kindness."
- "I love and accept myself unconditionally."

- "I radiate love and positivity from within."
- "I am enough just as I am."
- "I embrace my uniqueness and value it."

SUMMARY

"Love Yourself First" underscores the significance of self-love as a foundation for your well-being and healthy relationships. It encourages recognizing your worth, embracing strengths and weaknesses, and attending to physical, mental, and emotional needs. By prioritizing self-love, you can cultivate emotional resilience, confidently pursue personal growth, and find happiness. Occasional "selfishness" for self-care is healthy as it helps set boundaries and make decisions aligned with your values, ultimately enabling you to have a more profound impact on yourself and those around you.

STAY TRUE TO WHO YOU ARE

Protect yourself: Stay true to who you are and the choices you make. If you decide to be happy today, don't let outside negativity affect you. Take control of your mood and don't allow anyone or anything to steal your happiness. Imagine yourself as a superhero wearing a cape, and if necessary, create an invisible shield to block out negative influences.

"HAPPINESS IS NOT
SOMETHING READY-MADE.
IT COMES FROM
YOUR OWN ACTIONS."

DALAI LAMA

CHAPTER 10

THE HAPPY POWER HOUR

You've probably heard about successful people who have a structured morning routine and wake up earlier than most. They use these early hours for personal growth and empowerment. This morning routine is about setting a positive tone for the day.

The Happy Power Hour is a dedicated hour of your morning, focusing on personal growth, self-reflection, and cultivating a positive mindset. This uninterrupted "me-time" is the foundation for clarity, purpose, and inner strength. To embrace this practice, you may need to adjust your morning habits and rise a bit earlier. Yet, the rewards are significant, as beginning your day with positivity can profoundly impact how it unfolds.

During the Happy Power Hour, you can engage in various activities, including journaling, meditation, gratitude practice, goal visualization, affirmations, exercise, or reading inspirational material. The specific activities depend on your preferences and goals. You invest in your well-being and personal growth by dedicating this time to yourself. It feels amazing and provides a solid start to the day, fostering clarity, purpose, and inner resilience. Over time, it becomes the foundation for your personal development journey.

Establishing a morning routine centered on self-love isn't an act of selfishness; it's a profound commitment to self-care that fortifies your well-being and empowers you to radiate positivity and make a meaningful difference in the world by starting your day on a positive note.

Morning routines vary from person to person, but the key is finding one that resonates with you. Some may start by lying in bed with their eyes closed, reflecting on gratitude, which can bring a smile before getting out of bed. Others may begin with meditation and visualization, envisioning a smooth day with a pleasant commute, a positive work environment, and successful outcomes. Incorporating manifesting and visualization empowers you to shape your reality actively.

To boost your morning routine, it is important to include physical activity such as walking, jogging, biking, or any exercise that suits you. Aim for 30 minutes of cardio to strike a good balance. Regular exercise benefits your physical health, uplifts your mood, and boosts your energy levels. It fosters a positive connection between your body and mind, promoting overall well-being. During your exercise, express gratitude, acknowledging and appreciating your body's capabilities and the beauty of the world around you. This combination of movement and gratitude creates a profound sense of well-being. Incorporating exercise into your morning routine sets the stage for a day filled with vitality and positivity.

The power of consistency is the key to unlocking the full potential of a healthy morning routine. Through the commitment to a routine that truly resonates with you, you will witness the transformative effects unfold in your life.

Discovering the right Happy Power Hour for your needs and preferences is essential. Explore activities and rituals aligned with your goals and values to find what feels authentic. Once you have identified your ideal routine, consciously decide to stick to it. Consistency is the key that unlocks the door to lasting change and growth. Embrace the power of repetition and make your morning routine a non-negotiable part of your daily life.

As you commit to your routine, observe how your life transforms. Notice the positive shifts in your mindset, energy levels, productivity, and overall well-being. Embrace the ripple effect that consistency creates, as the benefits of your morning routine extend beyond the early hours of the day and permeate every aspect of your life. The journey of personal growth and transformation is not a sprint but a marathon. You build the foundation for long-term success and fulfillment through the consistent practice of a healthy morning routine. Embrace the process, be patient with yourself, and celebrate the small victories along the way. Set the tone for how you show up in the world, navigate challenges, and embrace opportunities. By prioritizing consistency in your morning routine, you take ownership of your life and become an active participant in shaping your destiny.

ACTION ITEMS:

During the Happy Power Hour, you dedicate time to invest in your personal growth and well-being. This hour is designed to increase your physical energy, improve mental clarity, and cultivate a positive and empowered mindset to tackle the day's challenges. You can customize the activities and duration based on your preferences and goals. Consistency is key. You will experience a harmonious blend of strength and relaxation by prioritizing daily self-care. The routine typically includes several essential components:

- **30 Minutes of Physical Exercise:** To enhance your energy and vitality, it is crucial to begin your day with physical activity. This can involve engaging in cardiovascular exercises such as jogging, jumping on a rebounder, biking, dancing, or practicing yoga. These activities release endorphins and serotonin, promoting a positive mood and providing your brain with a healthy oxygen supply.
- **2 Minutes of Just Smiling:** Put on a smile, even if it feels forced, and maintain it for at least two minutes. Smiling activates the well-known feel-good hormones, creating a positive feedback loop in your body and mind. Releasing endorphins, serotonin, dopamine, and oxytocin will uplift your mood, reduce stress, and contribute to a sense of happiness and well-being.

- **10 Minutes of Focus on Gratitude:** Set aside 10 minutes to focus on gratitude during your routine. Take this time to reflect on the things you are grateful for in your life. By practicing gratitude daily, you cultivate a positive mindset and nurture a sense of appreciation.
- **5 Minutes of Quiet Reflection or Meditation:** Take 5 minutes for a peaceful reflection or meditation in your routine. This dedicated time allows you to find inner calm, reduce stress, and center yourself. You may incorporate visualization techniques during this period to enhance your experience.
- **20 Minutes of Personal Development:** Use this time to read, listen to audio programs, or watch motivational videos. It's an opportunity to expand your knowledge, gain inspiration, and grow personally.
- **Journaling:** Incorporate journaling into your routine by taking a few moments to write down things you are grateful for, affirmations and goals for the day. This practice allows you to reflect, express gratitude and set positive intentions for the day ahead.

SUMMARY

The "Happy Power Hour" is a purposeful morning routine designed to cultivate personal growth and foster a positive mindset. While it may require adjustments to your morning habits, its impact on your day is significant. This self-care ritual encompasses journaling, meditation, exercise, and reading. Prioritizing this routine is not selfish; it empowers you to impact the world positively. Consistency is vital for lasting change, leading to an improved mindset, increased energy, and enhanced productivity. Embracing this process allows you to take active control of your life.

"TAKE CARE OF YOUR BODY.
IT'S THE ONLY PLACE
YOU HAVE TO LIVE."

JIM ROHN

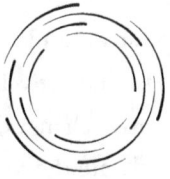

CHAPTER 11

NOURISH & MOVE

In today's fast-paced world, the remarkable synergy between healthy eating, physical activity, and the profound connection between a positive mindset and self-love has emerged as a powerful catalyst for personal transformation and overall well-being. In the present-day landscape, you must make your well-being a top priority because convenience often takes precedence over health. Embracing simplicity and mindfulness in your everyday life is critical to leading a healthier and more balanced life.

First and foremost, healthy eating and physical activity provide your body with the essential nutrients and energy it needs to function optimally. By nourishing yourself with wholesome foods, you support your physical health, strengthen your immune system, and enhance your vitality. Regular exercise not only improves your cardiovascular health and strengthens your muscles but also releases endorphins, serotonin, dopamine, and oxytocin, the "feel-good" cocktail that boosts your mood and reduces stress. It's your power fuel for a positive mindset.

But the benefits go beyond the physical realm. When you care for your body through healthy eating and physical activity, you also nurture your mind. Scientific research has shown that these practices profoundly impact cognitive function, memory, and mental clarity. By fueling your body with nutritious foods and engaging in exercise, you enhance your brain health, improve focus, and promote positive thinking.

Cultivating a positive mindset and actively working on your karmic impact can bring about transformative changes, raising your energy vibration significantly. This shift will accelerate the manifestation of your goals and desires. However, it's crucial to maintain a healthy body and mind throughout this journey. Karma, in its simplest form, implies that your actions have consequences. When you make conscious choices to prioritize your health through nourishing food and exercise, you are creating positive karma for yourself, and you are practicing self-love at the same time. By taking care of your body, you are sowing the seeds of well-being and vitality, which will manifest in various aspects of your life.

As you prioritize fostering a healthy mind and body synergy, try engaging in cardiovascular exercise amidst the beauty of natural surroundings. This harmonious connection with nature enhances your physical well-being and nurtures your mental and emotional health. Deepening your bond with nature is a profound way to reconnect with yourself. When you immerse yourself in outdoor workouts, take the opportunity to cultivate gratitude and recite affirmations. Repetitively affirming your intentions while walking or running creates a powerful resonance that the Universe joyfully responds to.

ACTION ITEMS:

Embrace the power of nutritious food and regular exercise to cultivate a balanced and vibrant life.

- **Recognize the Sacred Connection:** Understand that the bond between your mind, body, and energy is profound and deserves respect. Recognize that what we think, eat, and do impacts our lives. It extends beyond you and reflects the concept of karma, where your actions hold significance.

- **Choose Ethical Sourcing:** Opt for ethically sourced animal products over supporting mass production. This aligns you with principles of kindness and compassion while promoting the humane treatment of animals and sustainable farming.
- **Embrace Simplicity in Your Diet:** Simplify your diet by selecting foods with clear, easy-to-understand ingredients. Focus on unprocessed, whole foods like fruits, vegetables, whole grains, and nuts. These foods are rich in vitamins, minerals, and fiber, enhancing your health. Stay away from processed foods and carefully examine ingredient lists. If you're unsure about what's in your food, it's best to avoid eating it.
- **Practice Moderation:** Regarding animal products, practice moderation and mindful choices. Consume meat and fish once or twice a week, and consider reducing or eliminating dairy. Cow's milk is designed for calves, not humans, and reducing dairy will lead to better overall health.
- **Maintain Balance:** To maintain balance, reduce the intake of acidic substances such as caffeine, sugar, alcohol, nicotine, and drugs. Prioritize alkaline-forming foods like leafy greens, almonds, avocados, and citrus fruits, which should constitute at least 70% of your diet.
- **Stay Hydrated:** Ensure you stay hydrated by drinking 2-3 liters of pure water infused with a hint of lemon or cucumber daily. Hydration plays a critical role in detoxification and overall well-being.
- **Mindful Eating:** When you eat, it's not just about selecting the right foods but also about savoring and fully enjoying each bite. Be present during your meals, relish the experience, and focus on your body's hunger and fullness cues. This fosters a deeper connection to your food and its impact on your body and emotions.
- **Exercise Regularly:** Make sure to exercise regularly by dedicating five sessions of at least 30 minutes each week to moderate-intensity aerobic workouts or two and a half hours to vigorous-intensity exer-

cise, in addition to strength training. Select the sport that brings you joy and fun, ensuring you'll stay committed to it. Try to work out in nature as much as possible.

- **Practice Journaling before Bed:** Journaling will help you unwind and release stress. You can reflect on your day, gain valuable insights, and foster self-discovery. Setting intentions for the next day also creates clarity and a focused mindset. By emptying your mind and promoting relaxation, journaling improves your sleep quality.
- **Rest and Sleep:** Ensure 7-9 hours of restorative sleep each night for physical and mental health.

SUMMARY

Prioritizing well-being in today's fast-paced world involves recognizing the profound connection between healthy eating, physical activity, a positive mindset, and self-love. Healthy eating and regular exercise provide essential nutrients and physical health benefits and enhance cognitive function and mental clarity. Nurturing your body and mind through these practices aligns with positive karma, creating a ripple effect of well-being in various aspects of life.

THE BENEFITS OF SUPERFOODS:

Incorporate Superfoods into your daily diet to boost your health. These nutrient-dense foods are packed with vitamins, minerals, antioxidants, and other beneficial compounds. Superfoods offer exceptional health benefits, supporting overall well-being and contributing to a healthy diet. They can boost the immune system, promote heart health, improve brain function, enhance digestion, support weight management, and reduce inflammation.

Adding superfoods to your diet can significantly optimize your nutrition and support your overall health. This list showcases a selection of nutrient-dense superfoods, but there are many more options to explore. Including various foods in your meals can provide numerous health benefits.

Antioxidant-Rich Superfoods:
Blueberries
Goji berries
Raspberries
Dark chocolate (>70% cocoa)
Acai berries
Strawberries

Leafy Green Superfoods:
Spinach
Collard greens
Arugula
Kale
Beet greens
Romaine lettuce

Healthy Fat Superfoods:
Avocado
Flaxseeds
Olive oil
Salmon
Walnuts
Coconut oil

Protein-Packed Superfoods:
Quinoa
Lentils
Edamame
Greek yogurt
Chickpeas
Tofu

Fiber-Rich Superfoods:
Broccoli
Oats
Chia seeds
Brussels sprouts
Artichokes
Whole Grain Bread

Immune-Boosting Superfoods:
Citrus fruits
Ginger
Green tea
Garlic
Turmeric
Elderberries

"SURROUND YOURSELF
WITH ONLY PEOPLE
WHO ARE GOING TO
LIFT YOU HIGHER."

OPRAH WINFREY

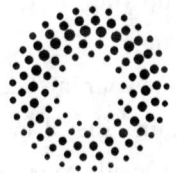

CHAPTER 12

YOUR PEERS

Ever heard the famous saying, "You are the average of the five people you spend the most time with"? It's often credited to the legendary motivational speaker and author Jim Rohn and carries a profound truth. This saying means that the people you choose to surround yourself with significantly impact your life's course. They influence your thoughts, behaviors, and where you're headed. Your peer group is critical to your personal growth and success recipe.

Picture your closest friends as mirrors reflecting back at you. Their attitudes, outlook on life, and mindset rub off on you. It's time to be picky about your inner circle. Steer clear of negative peers with clouds of gloom and doom over their heads, a consistently pessimistic mindset, and negative karma. Instead, embrace positivity and surround yourself with individuals who challenge and uplift you. Elevate your peer group. Seek out people who inspire you to aim higher.

Your peer group sets the standard for your growth because who you spend time with is who you become. If they're ahead of the curve, you've got the traction to level up. Proximity is your secret weapon. Diversity is your superpower. When your peers come from diverse backgrounds and experiences, it's like having a brainstorming session on steroids. They'll question your assumptions, flip your ideas around, and inspire creativity, innovation, and problem-solving.

Being with people who ignite your intellectual curiosity is like strapping on turbochargers for your brain. They'll introduce you to new concepts, offer invaluable insights, and provide constructive feedback. It's like a never-ending learning journey.

Now, here's the million-dollar question: Who's on your team? Are they pushing you to new heights or holding you back? If your current peers are not your dream team, seek out fresh peers who match your growth mindset. If finding these like-minded individuals feels like a challenge, consider mentors and coaches – the true North Stars of personal development. In their sessions, you can even discover your next-level peer group – people journeying towards a better mindset and a more fulfilling life.

Building these peer relationships isn't just great for your intellectual growth; it's your golden ticket. They'll introduce you to opportunities you never even dreamed of. Your network is about to explode with potential.

Understanding the importance of your peer group:

- **Different perspectives and ideas:** When you have a diverse group of peers, they bring different perspectives, experiences, and ideas. This diversity can broaden your thinking, challenge your assumptions, and help you see things from different angles. It encourages creativity, innovation, and problem-solving.

- **Continuous learning:** Being around people who challenge you intellectually and push you to expand your knowledge and skills can accelerate your learning. They can introduce you to new concepts, share valuable insights, and provide constructive feedback. This environment of continuous learning can help you stay motivated, adapt to new challenges, and help you grow both personally and professionally.

- **Accountability and support:** Surrounding yourself with supportive peers creates a positive and encouraging environment. They can provide emotional support, guidance and hold you accountable for your goals and aspirations. When faced with obstacles or self-doubt, having a network of supportive individuals can help you stay motivated, overcome challenges, and maintain a positive mindset.
- **Personal development:** Good peers can inspire and motivate you to become the best version of yourself. They can serve as role models, demonstrating qualities and behaviors you admire and aspire to. You can gain valuable insights and develop new skills by observing and learning from their successes and challenges.
- **Networking and opportunities:** Building strong peer relationships can open doors to new opportunities. They may introduce you to new connections, collaborations, or career prospects. By surrounding yourself with ambitious and driven individuals, you increase your chances of being exposed to new opportunities and expanding your network.

SUMMARY

Having good peers and surrounding yourself with people who challenge and support you is essential for personal and professional growth. They provide diverse perspectives, foster continuous learning, offer accountability and support, contribute to your personal development, and create networking opportunities. Choose your peers wisely and nurture those relationships to make a positive and impactful environment for your growth and success.

Setting Boundaries with Negative Peers in Your Circle

Establishing healthy boundaries is crucial when dealing with negative people in your circle of friends. It allows you to maintain your peace, happiness, and a positive mindset. Sometimes, on your journey to fulfillment, you may need to let go of peers whose energy vibration no longer aligns with yours. However, it's essential to approach this process with respect, responsibility, and a focus on your growth. Remember, what you put into the world will return to you, so avoid finger-pointing, resentment, or anger. Instead, gracefully let them go and stay true to your positive mindset and personal truth.

ACTION ITEMS:

Take a moment to assess your peer group and determine if the right circle of friends surrounds you or if you have to make adjustments.

Step 1: Reflect on Your Values and Goals

Take some time to reflect on your values, goals, and the kind of energy you want to surround yourself with. Consider how negative influences may impact your well-being and progress toward your goals. This self-reflection will help you gain clarity and motivation to set boundaries.

Step 2: Practice Mindfulness and Self-Awareness

Developing mindfulness and self-awareness is vital to recognizing the impact of negative energy on your well-being. When interacting with negative individuals, you pay close attention to your emotions, thoughts, and physical sensations. This heightened awareness will empower you to take proactive steps in setting boundaries. One technique you can try is visualizing an invisible shield that protects you from negative influences around such peers. Additionally, focus on positivity by silently reviewing your gratitude list or reminding yourself of positive aspects when they are present. By staying in your "Happy State", you can maintain your inner peace and protect yourself from the negativity around you.

Step 3: Assess the Impact of Negative Relationships

Evaluate the impact of specific relationships in your circle of friends. Identify individuals who consistently exhibit negative behavior, drain your energy, or hinder your personal growth. This assessment will help you prioritize which relationships require boundaries.

Step 4: Communicate Your Boundaries Clearly and Respectfully

When setting boundaries, it's essential to communicate your needs clearly and respectfully. Choose an appropriate time and place to have an open and honest conversation with the person in question. Express your feelings, concerns, and their negativity's impact on you.

When communicating your borders, it's important to use "I" statements to express your feelings and experiences without sounding accusatory. For example, instead of saying, "You always bring negative energy," you can use an "I" statement like, "I feel drained and overwhelmed when there is a lot of negativity around me." This way, you are sharing how their behavior impacts you personally without placing blame or attacking them. By using "I" statements, you can maintain a respectful and non-confrontational approach. It's crucial to disconnect from negative individuals and refrain from finger-pointing or judgmental language. Instead, prioritize your well-being and calmly express your needs and boundaries. Stay true to your karma. Effective communication is critical to setting boundaries while maintaining positive relationships.

Step 5: Set Clear Limits and Consequences

Establish clear limits on what behavior you will no longer tolerate. Communicate these limits to the person, emphasizing that you expect mutual respect wand positivity in the relationship. Discuss the consequences that will follow if the boundaries are repeatedly crossed.

Step 6: Surround Yourself with Positive Peers

Seek out and nurture relationships with positive, like-minded individuals who support your growth and well-being. Surrounding yourself with positive peers will create a supportive network that reinforces your positive mindset and helps you manifest your goals.

Step 7: Maintain your "Happy State" and Positive Mindset

Prioritize your "Happy State" and nurture a positive mindset by participating in activities that bring you joy, embracing gratitude, and fostering self-care practices. Doing so fortifies your resilience against negative influences and creates an environment that attracts greater positivity into your life.

Step 8: Practice Karma and Compassion

Even when disengaging from negative individuals, strive to maintain a sense of compassion and empathy. Wish them well on their journey and release negative emotions or resentment. Remember that practicing good karma involves treating others with kindness, even when setting boundaries.

> **PROJECTING**
>
> When you face criticism, negative feedback, or judgment from others, it's essential to recognize that their opinions and judgments reflect their own inner world. This phenomenon is known as "projecting." Projecting is a psychological defense mechanism where individuals unconsciously attribute their thoughts, emotions, or qualities to others. It occurs when someone displaces their insecurities, fears, or negative attributes onto another person, often to avoid confronting those aspects within themselves.

Remember, it's your choice how you respond, and it's crucial to ensure that others' thoughts, feelings, and judgments don't negatively impact you. People may express negativity about your choices because they make them uncomfortable or conflict with their values, or they might be triggered by fear. There are countless reasons someone might choose to be critical, but you can detach yourself from their opinions.

Detach, take a step back, and reflect on who is offering this criticism and why they are doing so. You possess the authority over your feelings; nobody else can control your emotional state. Nobody can harm you unless you grant them that power. Embrace your inner strength, rise above external judgments, and continue to make choices that align with your true self. Doing so gives you the resilience to navigate any storm with grace and self-assurance.

Surround yourself with Positivity

Surrounding yourself with positivity means intentionally creating an environment filled with positive energy, thoughts, and influences. It involves seeking out and embracing things, people, and experiences that uplift and inspire you while minimizing exposure to negativity and toxic influences.

- **Positive Mindset:** Cultivating a positive mindset involves focusing on the good, practicing gratitude, and reframing negative thoughts into more empowering ones. It means choosing to see challenges as opportunities for growth and maintaining an optimistic outlook on life.
- **Positive Relationships**: Surrounding yourself with positive relationships means seeking and nurturing connections with people who uplift, support, and inspire you. Positive relationships contribute to

your well-being and provide a sense of belonging and support.

- **Positive Environment:** Creating a positive environment involves surrounding yourself with things that bring joy, peace, and inspiration. It can include organizing your physical space, incorporating elements of nature, surrounding yourself with uplifting art or quotes, and creating a space that promotes relaxation and positivity.
- **Positive Media and Content:** Being mindful of the media and content you consume is important for maintaining a positive mindset. Choose to engage with media that inspires, educates, and uplifts you. This can include books, podcasts, movies, or social media accounts that promote positivity, personal growth, and well-being.
- **Positive Self-Care:** Prioritizing self-care and engaging in activities that nourish your mind, body, and soul is essential for surrounding yourself with positivity. This can include practicing mindfulness, engaging in hobbies you enjoy, exercising, eating nourishing foods, and taking time for rest and relaxation.

SUMMARY

By consciously surrounding yourself with positivity, you create an environment that supports your well-being, personal growth, and happiness. It helps to cultivate a positive mindset, build meaningful relationships, and create a life that aligns with your values and aspirations.

PART TWO

SETTING GOALS AND THE LAW OF ATTRACTION

"EVERYTHING IS ENERGY AND
THAT'S ALL THERE IS TO IT.
MATCH THE FREQUENCY
OF THE REALITY YOU WANT
AND YOU CANNOT HELP BUT
GET THAT REALITY IT CAN
BE NO OTHER WAY.
THIS IS NOT PHILOSOPHY.
THIS IS PHYSICS."

ALBERT EINSTEIN

CHAPTER 13

ENERGETIC VIBRATIONS

Energetic vibrations and frequencies are unseen forces that form the foundation of our existence. Everything in the Universe, including your thoughts and emotions, emits a distinct vibrational frequency, encompassing various aspects of personal growth and spiritual development.

When you project positive energy, you attract circumstances and individuals, resonating at a similar frequency. Conversely, negative energy results in undesirable experiences. By intentionally elevating your energetic vibrations through practices like gratitude, mindfulness, and self-care, you can raise your consciousness and draw higher vibrational experiences into your life. Aligning with positive vibrational energies magnetically draws more of your desired outcomes and positively impacts the world.

When spirituality meets quantum physics, we also encounter the concept of vibrational energy. In the quantum realm, particles are interconnected and responsive to observation. These particles can exhibit qualities of both solids and moving waves, which are called vibrations or frequency patterns. When an observer engages with these particles, they shift from wave-like to solid behaviors. This implies that your thoughts and intentions can genuinely affect how these particles behave, essentially blurring the line between you and what you observe. It also underscores the concept that everything in our surroundings is composed of vibrating energy.

As part of our conscious experience, our thoughts and emotions influence the energetic vibrations of the Universe. It's vital to be mindful of your thoughts, feelings, and intentions as they shape your interactions with the world. Both positive and negative thoughts hold significant power in this interconnected system.

Alignment with your vibrational energies means that your thoughts, emotions, and actions are in harmony with the positive energy you wish to attract. This entails aligning yourself with frequencies of abundance, joy, love, and success. It involves nurturing a positive mindset, emphasizing gratitude, and sustaining a high vibration while relinquishing negative thoughts, limiting beliefs, and self-doubt. When you align, you become receptive to opportunities and experiences that align with your desires.

Mindfulness, meditation, visualization, and affirmations are beneficial to achieve alignment. Surrounding yourself with positive influences, engaging in joy-inducing activities, and tending to your physical and emotional well-being also contribute to alignment. In the context of manifesting and a positive mindset, vibrational energy pertains to the frequency at which your thoughts, emotions, and beliefs resonate. A high vibrational state aligns with positivity, abundance, gratitude, and love, often accompanied by joy, enthusiasm, and optimism.

Consistently aligning with high vibrational energy enhances your ability to manifest your desires effectively. Your vibrational energy is intricately linked to your thoughts, emotions, beliefs, and actions, underscoring the importance of monitoring your thoughts diligently. Your thoughts shape your emotions, significantly affecting your energetic vibration and influencing your beliefs and actions. Therefore, maintaining awareness of your thoughts is crucial.

It is essential to be mindful and consciously shift your focus away from negative thoughts. Although it may require time and consistent effort, consistently directing your thoughts toward positivity will bring noticeable results over time. With practice, maintaining a positive mindset becomes easier and more natural.

When you operate at the highest vibrational frequency, you are essentially aligned with the Universe and your desires. This elevated state allows you to harness the power of the Law of Attraction more effectively and efficiently. Here's why:

- **Effortlessness:** At higher vibrational frequencies, things seem to flow effortlessly. This is because you are in sync with the Universe's natural order. Your intentions and desires align with the energy around you, making the manifestation process smoother. You encounter fewer obstacles and resistance on your path.

- **Belief:** When you vibrate at a high frequency, you inherently believe what you want to attract is already coming. This unwavering belief is crucial because it signals the Universe that you are ready to receive your desires. Your confidence acts as a magnet, drawing those desires closer to you.

- **Focus:** Maintaining a high vibrational frequency makes staying focused on your goals easier. Your energy naturally gravitates toward what you focus on and want to manifest, enhancing your concentration and determination. Distractions and doubts have less power over you, allowing you to stay on track with your intentions.

When you vibrate at a higher frequency, you create a harmonious relationship with the Law of Attraction. You become a co-creator with the Universe; your intentions are met with an open and responsive environment. It's like the Universe conspires to bring your desires to fruition because you align with its natural rhythm. So, focus on raising your vibrational frequency through positive thoughts, emotions, and actions, and watch how the Law of Attraction can work wonders in your life.

ACTION ITEMS:

Aligning with high vibrational energy is an ongoing practice. Consistency is key, and over time, you'll find it easier to maintain a positive mindset and attract abundance and positivity into your life:

- **Practice Gratitude Daily:** Begin and end your day by listing things you're grateful for. This simple practice shifts your focus to positive aspects of life and elevates your vibrational frequency.
- **Mindfulness Meditation:** Dedicate time each day to mindfulness meditation. This practice enhances self-awareness and helps you stay present, reducing negative thoughts and increasing your vibrational energy.
- **Visualization and Affirmations:** Create a vision board and use daily affirmations that align with your desires and goals. Visualizing and affirming positive outcomes raises your vibrational frequency and attracts what you want into your life.
- **Engage in Joyful Activities:** List activities that bring you joy and happiness. Incorporate these activities into your routine regularly to maintain a high vibrational state.
- **Surround Yourself with Positivity:** Choose to spend time with people who radiate positivity and support your well-being. Positive influences can help maintain your vibrational energy at a higher level.
- **2 Minutes of Just Smiling:** Put on a smile, even if it feels forced, and maintain it for at least two minutes. Smiling activates the well-known feel-good hormones, creating a positive feedback loop in your body and mind. Releasing endorphins, serotonin, dopamine, and oxytocin will uplift your mood, reduce stress, and contribute to a sense of happiness and well-being.
- **Self-Care:** Prioritize self-care by taking care of your physical and emotional well-being. Eat nourishing foods, exercise regularly, and get enough rest. A healthy body and mind contribute to a positive vibrational state.

What is Alignment?

What is alignment? In personal development, alignment refers to the state of harmoniously aligning your thoughts, beliefs, values, actions, and goals. It involves creating congruence between your inner self and external actions, ensuring harmony, and working towards a common purpose. When you align, you experience a sense of reality, clarity, and purpose, which can lead to greater fulfillment and success in various areas of your life. Alignment allows you to tap into your true potential and live a life that is true to yourself.

> **SUMMARY**
>
> Vibrational energies are at the core of our existence. Everything in the Universe, including our thoughts and emotions, emits distinct vibrational frequencies. Elevating your vibrations through practices like gratitude and mindfulness aligns you with positivity, making it easier to manifest your desires with the Law of Attraction. High vibrations lead to effortless flow, unwavering belief in your goals, and enhanced focus, creating a harmonious relationship with the Universe for prosperous manifestation.

EXUDE GOOD ENERGY EVERY DAY

I stepped into the bustling coffee shop on a rainy Monday morning at 7:30 am. The weather outside seemed to mirror the collective mood inside. Patrons were soaked from the rain, and the atmosphere was heavy with Monday morning blues. Even the employees behind the counters wore expressions of impatience and moodiness.

Customers jostled and pushed one another, their impatience palpable as they waited for their turn. In line before me stood an elderly lady struggling to find her wallet. The cashier, growing increasingly impatient, waited for her payment. Unfortunately, the people around her began making unkind comments about how she was holding everyone up, emphasizing that they had to rush off to work. The lady's distress was evident as she looked at the cashier and said, "I think I forgot my wallet, and now I can't bring the pastries to my friend's house. They are waiting for me."

The comments grew harsher, and the situation escalated. The lady behind the counter lowered the pastries, annoyed, shaking her head because the woman couldn't pay. I couldn't stand by any longer. I squeezed past the elderly lady and told the cashiers I would cover her pastries' cost.

The elderly lady stood there in shock, and the cashier asked incredulously, "You're doing what?" I replied, "I'll pay for her pastries so she can go see her friends right now." At that moment, the entire energy in the coffee shop underwent a profound transformation. Silence fell, and everyone listened intently to what was unfolding before them.

Once the ladies behind the counter understood the situation, their expressions softened, and they smiled. The atmosphere shifted, and a woman in the back exclaimed loudly, "There is still goodness in this world! Thank you for what you're doing." The elderly lady had tears in her eyes as she expressed her gratitude to me. I welled up with emotion, as did those around us, and we all felt the positive energy that had touched each and every one of us. As I squeezed my way out, people patted me on the shoulder and thanked me for my kindness. It was a genuinely memorable Monday morning, and in that moment, I felt an overwhelming sense of warmth and fulfillment.

"THE BIGGEST ADVENTURE
YOU CAN TAKE IS TO LIVE
THE LIFE OF YOUR DREAMS."

OPRAH WINFREY

CHAPTER 14

DREAM BIG

What do you truly desire? When you're on the path to becoming the best version of yourself, embracing a positive mindset, cultivating good karma, and permitting yourself to chase your dreams, that's when you need to unleash the power of dreaming big.

To "dream big" means harboring ambitious and expansive aspirations for your life. It's about setting lofty targets, allowing your imagination to paint grand possibilities, and aiming for achievements that might seem beyond your grasp. Bid farewell to fear and shed any limiting beliefs. Think of it as the genie in the bottle; ask yourself what you genuinely want, regardless of size. Dreaming big entails thinking beyond constraints, fully embracing your untapped potential, and pursuing your passions with unwavering courage and determination.

Dreaming big necessitates breaking free from self-imposed boundaries and defying societal expectations. It demands your willingness to step out of your comfort zone and take risks in pursuing extraordinary goals. It's all about challenging yourself, pushing boundaries, and relentlessly striving for personal and professional growth.

When you dream big, you unlock your creativity, imagination, and vision for the future. Set audacious goals that ignite your inspiration and motivation, and then take relentless action. Dreaming big leads you to a profound sense of purpose, fulfillment, and a life harmonizing with your deepest passions and desires.

So, dare to dream big, devise a meticulous plan, take determined action, and persevere through every challenge that comes your way.

Embrace this new mindset that bolsters your belief in your boundless potential, beckons opportunities, and fuels your pursuit of passions with unwavering resolve. It's about daring to envision a life beyond the present boundaries and having the audacity to chase those dreams with unbridled enthusiasm and unwavering resilience. Pursuing dreams involves setting specific goals, creating a plan, and consistent effort.

Dream big, set audacious goals, and have unshakable faith in your capacity to make them a reality. Let your dreams guide your journey toward a life of profound purpose, boundless fulfillment, and extraordinary achievements.

ACTION ITEMS:

Dream Exploration. Take this self-discovery and dream exploration journey to clarify your aspirations in various aspects of life. Your dreams are the stepping stones to a purposeful and fulfilling future.

When exploring your dreams, ask yourself: Which dream have you decided to pursue? What is the reason behind your choice of this dream? Then, take a moment to envision this dream becoming a reality. What do you see, sense, and feel in this future scenario? What is the best possible outcome from this dream coming true?

To gain clarity, go through the following steps for every dream separately.

- **Health and Well-being:** Envision your ideal state of health and well-being. What physical and mental aspects do you want to improve or maintain?
- **Family and Relationships:** Define your aspirations for family life

and relationships. How do you envision nurturing and strengthening these connections?

- **Personal Growth:** Explore your desires for personal growth and development. What skills, knowledge, or qualities do you want to cultivate?
- **Travel and Adventure:** Picture the places you dream of visiting and the adventures you want to experience. Where does your wanderlust lead you?
- **Hobbies and Passions:** Identify your interests and passions. What hobbies or activities bring you joy and fulfillment?
- **Emotional Resilience and Happiness:** Reflect on your emotional well-being. How can you enhance your resilience and cultivate lasting happiness?
- **Community Involvement:** Consider your role in the community. What contributions or initiatives do you want to be a part of?
- **Spiritual and Mindful Living:** Delve into your spiritual journey and mindfulness practices. How can you align your life with these principles?
- **Financial Success and Stability:** Envision your financial future. What level of success and stability do you aim to achieve?
- **Material Goals and Assets:** Define your material aspirations. What possessions or assets are essential to you?
- **Professional and Career Achievements:** Set career goals and achievements. Where do you see yourself professionally in the future?
- **Educational Pursuits:** Explore your desire for ongoing education. What knowledge or qualifications do you want to acquire?
- **Networking and Relationship Building:** Consider your social and professional networks. How can you expand and nurture these connections?
- **Entrepreneurship and Business Ventures:** Contemplate entrepre-

neurial endeavors. What business ventures or innovations are on your horizon?

- **Work-Life Balance and Well-being:** Prioritize work-life balance and overall well-being. How can you create harmony in your daily life?
- **Contribution and Impact:** Reflect on your desire to make a positive impact. What contributions or changes do you aspire to bring to the world?

SUMMARY

"Dream Big" is a call to embrace ambitious targets and set lofty goals for self-improvement. It encourages breaking free from limitations, shedding fear and doubts, and pursuing your passions with unwavering determination. Dreaming big unlocks your creativity, ignites your inspiration, and leads to a life of purpose and fulfillment.

THE 50 MILLION DOLLAR QUESTION.

When you are stuck in uncovering your most audacious dreams, you can engage with the "50 Million Dollar question." This powerful tool can help overcome limiting beliefs that may hinder exploring your true desires. Imagine a magical fairy has deposited 50 million dollars into your checking account, completely tax-free. Allow yourself to immerse in this newfound financial freedom's joy, relief, and happiness. Now, ask yourself: What would you do with this money? What is your next step? Why are you taking this step? Is it buying a house, going on a dream vacation, contributing to charity, or building a business? This exercise is a powerful tool to gain clarity and uncover your true aspirations. It helps bring your dreams into focus, guiding you toward the path that aligns with your deepest desires.

"SETTING GOALS IS
THE FIRST STEP IN
TURNING THE INVISIBLE
INTO THE VISIBLE."

TONY ROBBINS

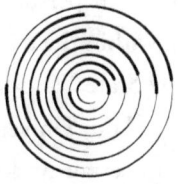

CHAPTER 15

GOAL SETTING

Armed with the understanding that your thoughts and emotions wield the power to shape your reality, it becomes evident that setting clear and specific goals is of utmost importance. The Law of Attraction will attract back to you what you wish for. Your task is to be exceptionally clear about what you desire. If you cannot attain clarity, the Law of Attraction cannot deliver what you want. Sending out conflicting frequencies will only draw in inconsistent and unsatisfying results. When setting your goals, it's vital to possess a clear understanding of your desires. Write your goals in intricate detail, and commit to reviewing them regularly to maintain your focus and motivation. Engage in this effort, let go of all limiting beliefs, and ask yourself the two pivotal questions: What do I want? And why do I want it?

Establishing goals is instrumental in fostering personal and professional growth. When you attach strong reasons to the goals you set, they become more attainable and manageable. The underlying motivations behind your goals serve as powerful tools. Therefore, when you embark on goal-setting, ask yourself, "Why do I want this?" When you are clear about what you want and why you want it, you ignite a powerful force that propels you forward. Your goals act as a guiding path, enabling progress tracking and the eventual manifestation of your desired results.

With the Law of Attraction, your personal genie—you can achieve, become, or accomplish anything within the realm of your imagination. Wear a smile, step into your "Happy State," and let the flow guide you toward your goals. You are the Master of Your Universe; anything you can imagine is possible. Beware, though; if uncertainty clouds your wishes, exercise caution. The Law of Attraction faithfully reflects your predominant thoughts. Focus on what you desire, and avoid dwelling on things you wish to avoid.

Embrace the power of positive thinking and maintaining a high vibrational state. Visualization is key- visualizing your goals as they have already been achieved. With this process, we program our subconscious minds to align with our goals, making them feel more attainable and tangible. This technique also helps to build motivation and belief in your ability to attain your goals. You can expedite the manifestation process by focusing on the positive facets of your goals and feeling gratitude as they are accomplished. Craft vivid mental imagery involving all your senses to intensify this process. Dedicate ten minutes daily to visualize your goals and immerse yourself in the joy and excitement of their fulfillment. Say, "Thank you, Universe".

A valuable tool to consider is a vision board consisting of a collage of images, words, and phrases that symbolize your aspirations. You can curate a collection that reflects your desires by browsing magazines or printing out relevant materials. When you select and arrange images and words that represent your goals, it forces you to clarify precisely what you want. When you consistently focus your thoughts and emotions on these visual representations, you can align your energy, raise your vibrational frequency, and become more aligned with your desires and the things you want to manifest. Place your vision board in a prominent location where you can frequently gaze upon it.

Setting clear and compelling goals is essential for achieving success in any area of life. Vague goals like "I want to be successful" are less effective than specific goals like "I want to increase my income by 20 percent in the next year." Your goals should be clear, measurable, achievable, relevant, and time-bound (SMART goals).

You can magnetize opportunities to manifest your dreams by consistently aligning your thoughts, emotions, and actions. Ask for what you desire, have faith in its manifestation, and it shall be granted. Picture this: Armed with a positive mindset and empowering beliefs, you're not merely wishing for success but confidently expecting it. The Universe conspires by aligning circumstances, people, and opportunities to facilitate your journey toward realizing your dreams. It's not magic; it's the Law of Attraction in action. Ultimately, the goal is to shift your thoughts, emotions, and beliefs to align with the reality you want to create.

ACTION ITEMS:

Please take out your journal and ask yourself what you truly want and, most importantly, why you want it. Separate your desires into two categories: personal and professional success.

SMART Goals:

Use this framework to ensure your goals are well-defined and more likely to be achieved successfully.

- **Specific:** Specify your goals.
- **Measurable:** Determine how you'll measure your progress and recognize when you've achieved them.
- **Attainable:** Ensure your goals are realistic and achievable.
- **Relevant:** Validate that your goals align with your values and long-term objectives.
- **Time-Bound:** Set a deadline for reaching your goals.

Chunking:

Divide larger goals into manageable, bite-sized steps or milestones. This approach will help you mitigate overwhelm and foster a sense of accomplishment.

Taking Action:

To realize your goals, go above and beyond conventional efforts. Refrain from passive waiting. Get up and move. Action is the conduit through which the Universe brings forth circumstances and synchronicities to fulfill your dreams.

Visualization:

Embrace the practice of envisioning your goals as already accomplished. This technique cultivates motivation and bolsters your belief in your ability to attain them.

Positive Psychology:

It is crucial to maintain a positive mindset, focusing on the rewards and benefits of achieving your goals rather than dwelling on potential obstacles or failures. When you encounter challenges, remember to focus more on your goals than on the obstacles you're dealing with.

Emotional Mastery:

Harness control over your emotions, recognizing their profound impact on your motivation and focus. What you emit into the Universe, you shall receive. Thus, remain in your "Happy State," keep your positive karma, and have faith that all your dreams shall manifest.

The Vision Board:

The key is to use the vision board as a focal point for your thoughts and emotions, consistently aligning yourself with your goals and desires.

- **Clarify Your Goals**: Selecting and arranging images and words that represent your desires forces you to clarify exactly what you want.
- **Stay Focused**: Having your Vision Board prominently displayed where you can see it daily is a constant reminder of your goals. It helps you stay focused on what you want to attract into your life.

- **Elevate Your Vibration**: By regularly looking at your Vision Board and feeling the emotions associated with your goals, you raise your vibrational frequency and become more aligned with your desires.
- **Boost Visualization**: Visualization is a critical component of the Law of Attraction. A Vision Board is a powerful visualization tool that allows you to see your goals as if they have already been achieved.
- **Increase Belief and Positivity**: Creating and looking at your Vision Board can boost your belief that your goals are attainable. It encourages a positive mindset and an optimistic outlook.

SUMMARY

Goal setting is a powerful tool for shaping your reality and harnessing the Law of Attraction. To manifest your desires effectively, clarity is essential—write your goals in intricate detail and review them regularly to maintain focus and motivation. Setting clear and compelling goals, like SMART goals, propels personal and professional growth, guiding toward achieving desired results. Embracing positive thinking, visualization, maintaining a high vibrational state, and creating a Vision Board aligns your energy with your goals and accelerates the manifestation process.

ARE YOU LIVING IN A FANTASY WORLD?

Fantasies, dreams, and goals differ in terms of action and attainability:

Fantasy:
Fantasies are often unrealistic desires without a clear plan. They involve wishful thinking but lack commitment to action. Typically, fantasies remain in the realm of imagination with no concrete steps toward realization.

Dream:
Dreams are deeply desired, realistic outcomes imbued with passion and significance.

They require effort and action rooted in personal values and aspirations.

Pursuing dreams involves setting specific goals, creating a plan, and consistent effort.

Goal:
Goals are specific, measurable, and time-bound steps toward realizing dreams. They have well-defined criteria for success and a clear action plan.

Achieving goals involves breaking down dreams into manageable tasks, requiring disciplined and systematic effort.

Fantasies lack action and practicality, while dreams and goals involve clear intentions and actionable steps, with goals serving as the practical milestones toward realizing your dreams.

"YOU ARE THE MASTER OF YOUR DESTINY. YOU CAN INFLUENCE, DIRECT, AND CONTROL YOUR OWN ENVIRONMENT. YOU CAN MAKE YOUR LIFE WHAT YOU WANT IT TO BE."

NAPOLEON HILL

CHAPTER 16

LIMITING BELIEFS VS EMPOWERING BELIEFS

In your journey of personal growth and self-discovery, you will often encounter the clash between limiting beliefs and empowering beliefs. Limiting beliefs are the self-imposed barriers that hold you back from reaching your full potential. They are the thoughts and perceptions that undermine your confidence, hinder your progress, and restrict your possibilities. On the other hand, empowering beliefs are the transformative beliefs that propel you forward, fuel your resilience, and unlock your true capabilities. By understanding the power of your beliefs and learning to challenge and replace limiting beliefs with empowering ones, you can break free from self-imposed limitations and embrace a life of limitless potential.

First, meet the not-so-welcome guests: limiting beliefs. Think of them as outdated software running in your mind, holding you back from your full potential. They tend to be rather pessimistic, like a rain cloud on a sunny day. These beliefs are the culprits behind those self-defeating thoughts, like "I can't do it" or "I'm not worthy." Sound familiar? They're the chains that keep you tethered to your comfort zone, even if it's uncomfortable.

Now, let's introduce their more uplifting counterparts: empowering beliefs. Picture them as personal life coaches who say, "You've got what it takes!" Empowering beliefs are like jet fuel for your aspirations. They fill you with confidence, resilience, and the motivation to take action.

The real difference? Limiting beliefs are like heavy anchors, weighing you down with doubt and keeping you in familiar but limited territory. On the other hand, empowering beliefs are like boosters, propelling you forward with unwavering self-assurance. Here's the exciting part: you can transform your limiting beliefs into empowering ones. Think of it as a mental renovation project. Start by recognizing those outdated beliefs and challenging their validity. Are they based on facts or simply old stories you've been telling yourself? Then, gather evidence that supports your empowering beliefs. You can even practice positive affirmations and self-talk to reinforce them.

But remember, this isn't a quick fix; it's a process. Changing beliefs takes time, introspection, and consistent effort. You might need to confront beliefs you've held onto for a long time. But here's the silver lining: it's a journey that leads to personal growth and fulfillment.

In the end, empowering beliefs is your secret weapon. They light the path to your potential and success. By embracing them, you'll unlock your full capabilities and craft a life filled with purpose and achievement. So go ahead, embark on that empowering belief transformation journey, and watch your life transform along with it!

> At times, limiting beliefs can be deeply ingrained and resistant to change, embedded within our belief system for a significant period. If you find it challenging to address these beliefs on your own, seeking the guidance of a professional therapist or hypnotist can be a valuable option. They possess the expertise and tools to help undo and overcome these stubborn limiting beliefs, facilitating a transformative journey towards personal growth and empowerment.

Limiting Beliefs: The following are a few examples of common limiting beliefs that will hold you back from reaching your full potential. Identifying and challenging these beliefs is essential to your personal growth and self-improvement.

- "I'm not good enough."
- "I don't deserve success."
- "I'm not smart/talented enough."
- "I'm afraid of failure."
- "I'll never be able to change."
- "I don't have enough time/money/resources."
- "Others are better than me."
- "I can't do it."

Empowering beliefs: These beliefs form a solid foundation for cultivating a positive mindset, elevating your self-confidence, and empowering you to take bold steps toward your cherished goals and dreams. They stand by your side as you grow personally, strengthening your resilience and nurturing an unwaveringly positive mindset.

- "I am capable of achieving anything I set my mind to."
- "I am just as deserving of success as anyone else."
- "I am enough."
- "I am smart and talented."
- "I have the power to create positive change in my life."
- "I am worthy of love and respect."
- "I am resilient and can overcome any obstacle."
- "I embrace failure as an opportunity for growth and learning."
- "I am deserving of abundance and prosperity."

Unearthing limiting beliefs is a continuous journey of self-discovery. Embrace patience and self-compassion as you courageously confront and dismantle these barriers. Through your newfound awareness, you pave the way to replace them with empowering beliefs that fuel your relentless ascent toward growth and triumph. These empowering beliefs, once cultivated, serve as potent daily affirmations and incantations, igniting your path to greatness.

ACTION ITEM:

Identifying limiting beliefs is an empowering process that requires self-reflection and introspection. Here are some steps to help you recognize and uncover your own limiting beliefs:

- **Self-awareness:** Cultivate self-awareness by focusing on your thoughts, emotions, and behaviors. Notice any recurring patterns or negative self-talk that may be holding you back.
- **Question your beliefs:** To tackle limiting beliefs, you can ask yourself the following questions:

    a. What beliefs do I hold about myself and my abilities?

    b. Are these beliefs based on evidence and facts, or are they assumptions or interpretations?

    c. How do these beliefs impact my thoughts, emotions, and actions?

    d. Are there any past experiences or influences that have contributed to the formation of these beliefs?

    e. Are there alternative perspectives or counterexamples that challenge these limiting beliefs?

    f. What evidence or experiences contradict these beliefs?

    g. How would my life be different if I let go of these limiting beliefs?

    h. What new empowering beliefs can I adopt to replace the limiting ones?

- **Explore your comfort zone:** Step outside of your comfort zone and explore new experiences. Notice any resistance or fear, as it may indicate underlying limiting beliefs.
- **Journaling:** Take the time to engage in reflective journaling and allow yourself to explore your thoughts and beliefs. Write down any self-limiting beliefs that come to mind and examine their origins and their impact on your life. This process of introspection will provide valuable insights into the patterns and beliefs that may hold you back. Once identified, consciously choose to empower beliefs to replace the self-limiting ones. By consistently journaling and reinforcing these empowering beliefs, you can create a positive shift in your mindset and pave the way for personal transformation and manifesting your desires.
- **Seek feedback:** Reach out to trusted friends, mentors, or coaches who can provide objective insights and help you identify any limiting beliefs influencing your mindset.
- **Notice your language:** Pay attention to your language when discussing yourself or your abilities. Are there any recurring negative phrases or self-deprecating statements that reflect limiting beliefs?
- **Core values and goals:** Reflect on your core values and long-term goals. Are there any beliefs that contradict or hinder your progress toward these aspirations?

SUMMARY

Beliefs shape your journey: limiting beliefs hold you back like anchors, while empowering beliefs act as jet fuel, boosting your confidence and motivation. Transform limiting beliefs into empowering ones through introspection, challenging their validity, and practicing positive affirmations. It's a progression that leads to personal growth and fulfillment, guiding you toward success and purpose.

Challenge one limiting belief or pattern at the time and answer the following questions:

1. Define your limiting belief or pattern:

   _____
   _____
   _____
   _____

2. What will it cost you if you don't change this?

   _____
   _____
   _____
   _____

3. Write down 10 reasons why it is crucial to change this belief or pattern now.

_____
_____
_____
_____
_____
_____
_____
_____

4. Create a comprehensive list of all the positive outcomes and pleasures you will experience once you have transformed this belief or pattern. How will you feel?

_____
_____
_____
_____
_____
_____
_____
_____
_____

Interrupt the pattern when the old belief arises:

- **Awareness:** Be aware of when the limiting belief arises and consciously accept its presence. Visualize a stop sign in your mind and firmly say "Stop" to interrupt the pattern.

- **Change your perspective:** Challenge the belief by replacing it with more positive thoughts. Keep in mind the list of pleasures you have identified to reinforce your new mindset.

- **Visualization:** Imagine yourself breaking free from the pattern and visualize the positive outcomes that come with it. Feel the pleasure you will gain.

- **Action:** Take small steps towards applying new behaviors and beliefs that align with your desired change

"THE LAW OF ATTRACTION STATES THAT WHATEVER YOU FOCUS ON, THINK ABOUT, READ ABOUT, AND TALK ABOUT INTENSELY, YOU'RE GOING TO ATTRACT MORE OF INTO YOUR LIFE."

JACK CANFIELD

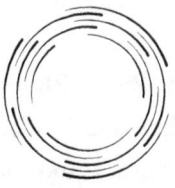

CHAPTER 17

THE LAW OF ATTRACTION

The Law of Attraction is a powerful cosmic force that governs the entire Universe, shaping every moment and experience in your life. Regardless of your identity or location, this mighty law molds your life through your thoughts. You catalyze the Law of Attraction's action primarily through your thoughts.

The Law of Attraction is based on the fact that your thoughts and emotions emit a particular energy frequency or vibration that aligns with similar energies in the Universe. Your thoughts and emotions have a magnetic quality, attracting into your life experiences and circumstances that resonate with your predominant mental and emotional states. Positive or negative thoughts and emotions attract corresponding positive or negative experiences into your life.

Much like karma, which serves as a reminder that our actions, thoughts, and intentions ripple through the Universe, similar to dropping a stone into a pond. These ripples return to us, shaping our present and future encounters. When your actions align with a positive mindset and empowering beliefs, you initiate a cycle of positivity and goodness that circles back to you. You are vibrating on the level of positivity and infinite potential.

Think of Karma as the Universe's way of maintaining balance. Think of the Law of Attraction as the Universe fulfilling all your dreams and wishes.

The Genie Analogy: In "The Secret," Rhonda Byrne uses the genie analogy in the bottle to illustrate how the Law of Attraction works. According to her, our thoughts are like wishes, and the Universe (or the Law of Attraction) is like the genie. When we focus on our desires and have a clear intention, it's as though we're making a wish to the Universe. In the genie analogy and the Law of Attraction, the Universe responds to our requests (wishes) or thoughts. If our thoughts are positive and aligned with our desires, the Universe will respond by bringing those desires into our lives.

Within Metaphysical and Spiritual Discourse: The Law of Attraction is widely regarded as a fundamental law governing our Universe. This profound concept has left an indelible mark on the annals of human history, with numerous prominent figures from various epochs incorporating it into their teachings and writings. Notably, luminaries such as the ancient Greek philosopher Socrates acknowledged the power of one's thoughts and their influence on the course of one's life. The Renaissance polymath Leonardo Da Vinci explored the interconnectedness of the human mind and the world, recognizing that our thoughts shape our reality.

Johann Wolfgang von Goethe, the literary genius, explored the human psyche and emotions, where he uncovered the intimate connection between thoughts, feelings, and the world's unfolding. In Quantum Physics, Max Planck and Albert Einstein made significant contributions that hinted at the idea that our thoughts, through vibrations or other mechanisms, influence matter.

These distinguished individuals, and many more, have integrated the principle of the Law of Attraction into their lessons and writings, regarding it as the most potent law governing the Universe. In their various fields of expertise, these luminaries understood that the Law of Attraction was not a mere philosophical or spiritual concept but an acknowledgment of the profound interplay between human consciousness and the world around us. It was the recognition that our thoughts, intentions, and beliefs, in many ways, govern our lives, shaping the reality we experience.

When harnessing the Law of Attraction, it's vital to concentrate on your desires rather than your fears. Your focus should be on what you want rather than what you don't want. Persistently fixating on the negatives in your life or dwelling on unfulfilled dreams will inadvertently draw more of the same into your existence. This is because the Law of Attraction operates on the principle that you manifest whatever occupies your predominant thoughts into your reality. Given that you naturally draw into your life the things you predominantly think about, it becomes evident which thoughts have dominated each area of your life.

Armed with the knowledge and insights you'll receive within the pages of this book, you possess the tools to transform your reality. You can bring forth the life you genuinely desire by aligning your thoughts and emotions with your aspirations. By directing your focus toward your desires instead of dwelling on what you wish to avoid, you can redirect the trajectory of the life you manifest, thus paving the way for abundance, happiness, and success.

To use the Law of Attraction to your advantage, you just need to focus on positive thoughts, visualizations, and emotions, and you will attract positive outcomes and experiences. By aligning your thoughts, emotions, and actions with what you want to attract, you can create a vibrational match and bring those desires into reality. The Law of Attraction is a universal principle that responds to your thoughts and beliefs. "Like attracts like," meaning that positive thoughts attract positive outcomes, and negative thoughts attract adverse outcomes. It is really that simple.

The Bible teaches that your requests will be granted when you ask with genuine belief. In Matthew 7:7-8 it states, "Ask, and you will receive; seek, and you will find; knock, and the door will be opened to you. For everyone who asks receives, and the one who seeks finds, and to the one who knocks, it will be opened." This verse encourages believers to approach God sincerely and trust that their requests will be answered.

Similar asking, believing, and receiving principles can be found in various religious and spiritual traditions, including Hinduism, Shamanism, Taoism, and the New Thought movement. This three-step process underscores that by asking the Universe for your desires, believing that they are already within your grasp, and being open to receiving them, you can attract positive outcomes into your life.

Ask: When it comes to setting goals, precision is vital. Instead of expressing a general desire like "I want to be rich," it's essential to be specific about the amount of money you aim to have, why you want it, and the timeline for achieving this goal. Similarly, when it comes to weight loss, don't just wish to "lose weight"; instead, you should state the exact number of pounds you wish to shed and set a target date, as this will provide clarity and focus. Whether in your personal or professional life, it's crucial to identify precisely what you want to achieve. By clearly defining your desires and asking empowering questions such as "What do I really want? And why do I want it?" and allowing yourself to answer without compromise, you can gain clarity on your true objectives.

Belief: Belief is a fundamental aspect of the Law of Attraction. Nurture empowering beliefs while eliminating limiting ones that may impede your progress. By adopting empowering beliefs and developing strong self-confidence, you can overcome obstacles and achieve your desired outcomes. Have faith that the Universe will deliver.

Receive: To receive, you must release fear, doubt, or limiting beliefs and be genuinely open to receiving. With this mindset, take the first step and act. Merely manifesting your desires and waiting at home is insufficient. To receive what you desire, you must consistently take action and remain open to opportunities and resources. Believe that you will encounter the right people and circumstances. You'll be amazed by the synchronicities the Universe orchestrates along your journey. Maintain a positive mindset of abundance, stay receptive to possibilities, and watch your biggest dreams and goals manifest before your eyes. It's both exciting and sometimes mind-boggling.

It's vital to prioritize the vibration or frequency you emit to harness the power of the Law of Attraction. If you ever feel trapped in negativity or stagnation, it's time to take charge and elevate your vibration to new heights. This empowering action plan presents you with a set of tools designed to help you vibrate at the highest frequency imaginable. Each tool corresponds to a specific chapter in this book, providing you with a comprehensive approach to transforming your mindset into a positive, high-frequency state. Embrace these tools and unlock the ability to manifest true beauty and abundance in your life.

As you embark on your empowering journey to utilize the Law of Attraction, starting by exploring these chapters and actively engaging in journaling is highly recommended. Writing has a remarkable impact, as it amplifies the power of your thoughts and intentions by 40%. So, grab your pen and paper, take diligent notes, and wholeheartedly participate in the exercises provided. You will witness a profound shift occurring within your entire being.

Never underestimate the immense significance of cultivating a positive mindset. It is the foundation upon which your manifestations thrive. Embrace unwavering faith and belief in the realization of your desires. Let go of all limiting beliefs that might hold you back. You are deserving of the outcomes you seek, and the Universe eagerly awaits you to fulfill your wishes swiftly and gracefully. Hold onto your dreams, for they are within reach, and trust in the magical power of your manifestation abilities.

ACTION ITEMS:

Having journeyed through Part I of this book and embraced the tools provided, your mindset should have undergone a profound transformation, resulting in an elevated energy level. As a result, tackling these action items should now feel effortless and natural for you.

Gratitude is the Foundation:

Gratitude is the fundamental cornerstone of your personal growth and attracts your desires into your life. It is the bedrock upon which you will build your journey towards a fulfilling and abundant life. By cultivating a grateful mindset, you open yourself to the immense power of appreciation and love. Gratitude allows you to shift your focus from what is lacking to what is present, fostering a deep sense of contentment and joy. Through gratitude, you will lay a solid foundation for your personal and spiritual growth, unlocking the limitless possibilities that await you on your path. Here's a simple practice to get you started:

- **Morning and Evening Gratitude:** Set aside a few moments each morning and evening to reflect on what you're grateful for. Write down ten things that you deeply appreciate in your life.
- **Celebrate Your Accomplishments:** Take time to acknowledge your personal victories. Jot down ten things that you have accomplished and feel proud of. Recognizing your achievements boosts your self-confidence and motivates you to strive for more.
- **Embrace Joyful Moments:** Recall ten things that brought you happiness and filled your heart with joy. It could be a kind gesture from a loved one, a beautiful sunset, or a scene filled with laughter. By appreciating these moments, you invite more joy into your life.

Daily Affirmations: The Power of Positive Self-Talk

Integrating positive affirmations into your daily routine will have a transformative effect on your mindset and overall well-being. By stating your desires as if they are already happening, you tap into the power of your subconscious mind:

- **Embrace the Present:** Frame your affirmations in the present tense as if your desires are already a reality. For example, say, "I am confident and successful," "I live a life of abundance," and "I am healthy and happy." By affirming these statements, you align your thoughts and beliefs with the life you want to manifest.

- **Repetition is Key:** Repeat your affirmations throughout the day, allowing them to sink deep into your subconscious mind. You rewire your thinking patterns and reinforce empowering beliefs by consistently reinforcing positive statements. Find moments during your day to silently or verbally repeat your affirmations.
- **Stay Engaged:** To keep your affirmations fresh and engaging, periodically introduce new ones into your practice. It prevents monotony and keeps your mind receptive to new possibilities. Experiment with affirmations that resonate with your current goals and aspirations.

Watch Your Thoughts:

- **Cultivate Mindfulness:** Kickstart a daily mindfulness routine. Observe your thoughts without judgment, allowing you to recognize negative thinking habits.
- **Swap Out Negative Thoughts and Limiting Beliefs:** Whenever you catch yourself in a negative thought, swiftly replace it with a positive one. When a negative thought pops up, say "Stop," flash a smile, be proud that you caught it, and replace it with an empowering affirmation.

Clarify Your Desires:

Clearly define what you want to attract into your life. Be specific and detailed about your goals, whether they are related to career, relationships, health, or personal growth. The more clarity you have, the easier it becomes to align your thoughts and actions with your desires.

- **Vision Board:** Create a vision board with images and words that represent your goals and desires. Place it where you can see it daily.

Elevate Your Energy:

- **Prioritize Self-Care:** Set aside time for activities that bring you joy and rejuvenation, whether exercising, pursuing hobbies, or simply relaxing. Remember, it's beautiful to prioritize self-love and self-care.
- **Surround Yourself with Positivity:** Invest time with individuals who radiate positivity and offer support. Minimize your exposure to negative influences, both in the media and in your social interactions. Be mindful of the company you keep, and limit time spent with individuals who frequently complain or drain your energy.
- **Nurture Positive Relationships:** Take a moment to reflect on your existing relationships. Invest in infusing them with positivity and establish healthy boundaries when necessary.
- **Practicing self-belief:** Cultivate a strong belief in yourself and your abilities to manifest your desires.

Visualization and Manifesting:

- **Visualization Exercise:** Manifesting and visualizing becomes more accessible when you locate a peaceful, interruption-free spot to sit in a relaxed posture. Close your eyes, inhale deeply through your nose into your belly, and exhale through your mouth to ease into a meditative state. Visualize your goals with utmost clarity, as though they've already become reality. Dedicate about 10 minutes to this practice each day. Engage deeply in the feelings of happiness and joy tied to your dreams and desires coming true. Feel the gratitude that wells up when your goals have materialized. Envision yourself radiating happiness adorned with a smile.

Take Inspired Action:

- **Create an Action Plan:** Break your goals into small, actionable steps. Start taking one small action each day towards your goals.

- **Follow Your Intuition:** Listen to your inner guidance. If something feels right, take action. Trust your instincts.

Overcoming Challenges:

As you begin your journey to harness the Law of Attraction, you must be aware of your self-talk and general attitude. Keep in mind that the Law of Attraction operates bidirectionally. This means that it brings into your reality whatever occupies your predominant thoughts. Reflect on these questions: Are you nurturing many positive and empowering thoughts, or are you entangled in negative thoughts and limiting beliefs? Picture it as a scale – do your positive thoughts tip the balance over the negative ones? Sometimes, all it takes is a few minor adjustments to tilt the scale towards positivity once more.

If this equilibrium is out of alignment, it might seem you're encountering hurdles on your path to manifesting your desires. Be candid with yourself. We generate approximately 60,000 thoughts each day. Make a conscious effort to ensure that most of these thoughts lean towards the positive and empowering side.

- **Resilience Building:** Develop strategies to bounce back from setbacks. Remember, challenges are part of the journey.
- **Consistency:** Ensure you're staying consistent with your daily practices. Adjust and refine your techniques as needed.

Review and Adjust:

- **Review Progress:** Look at your journal and stock your journey so far. Celebrate your wins and assess areas that need improvement.
- **Adjust Your Plan:** Modifying your action plan and goals is okay based on your progress and changing desires.

Embrace Patience and Trust:

- **Have Faith in the Process:** Trust that the Universe works in your favor, and practice patience. As Tony Robbins, the motivational speaker, likes to say: Life is not happening to you. Life is happening for you. Embrace the Law of Attraction with unwavering faith. Visualize yourself as unstoppable, firmly believing in your potential rather than entertaining doubt. See yourself as the creator and leader of your life, a force for good, and the guiding voice.
- **Embrace Opportunities:** Keep an open mind and remain receptive to new opportunities and possibilities that may cross your path.

SUMMARY

The Law of Attraction states that your thoughts and emotions create a magnetic energy that attracts corresponding experiences. Align thoughts with desires, stay positive, and believe in their manifestation. This universal principle is found in various cultures and religions. Ask, believe, and remain open to receiving. Precision, empowering beliefs, and action are crucial. Elevate your vibration, explore tools, and embrace journaling. Cultivate a positive mindset as it's essential for successful manifestations. Trust in your manifestation abilities.

"IMAGINATION IS EVERYTHING.
IT IS THE PREVIEW OF LIFE'S
COMING ATTRACTIONS."

ALBERT EINSTEIN

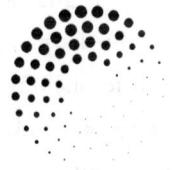

CHAPTER 18

MANIFESTING AND VISUALIZATION

Manifesting is all about you, your dreams, and your power to bring them into reality intentionally. It is the process of bringing your desires and goals into physical reality through the power of intention, belief, and alignment of thoughts and emotions. Your thoughts and emotions emit a specific energy or vibration that attracts corresponding experiences and circumstances into your life, and using this knowledge, you possess the incredible ability to shape the world around you. Manifesting is directly linked with the Law of Attraction, which means that what you hold in your heart and mind tends to materialize in your life.

To kickstart the manifesting process, start by setting a crystal-clear intention or goal. This means painting a detailed picture of what you want to manifest. Visualization is your trusty tool here. Imagine your desired outcome with such vividness that it feels like you've already achieved it. Engage all your senses, and let the emotions associated with your goal wash over you. By engaging your senses and feeling the emotions associated with your goal, you align your energy and vibration with what you want to attract. This act harmonizes your energy with what you're seeking.

It also calls for a positive mindset and unwavering belief in yourself. It's about releasing those limiting beliefs and doubts holding you back. Affirmations, uplifting self-talk, positive karma, and the practice of gratitude are your companions on this journey, helping you reinforce positive beliefs, maintain a positive, expectant mindset, and sustain a high vibration.

Manifesting involves not just your mental processes but also requires taking inspired actions toward your goals. It involves actively pursuing opportunities, making choices, and taking steps towards your desired outcome. By consistently aligning your thoughts, emotions, and actions with your goals, you can attract opportunities, people, and events that help you realize your desires and turn your goals into reality.

This process isn't about wishful thinking or waiting for things to happen magically. It requires personal responsibility and commitment, self-reflection, and consistent effort. It's a practice that spans all aspects of your life, from relationships and careers to health and personal growth. You have the power within you to manifest your dreams – the Universe is listening, and it's time to take the reins of your destiny.

> When stress and pressure to achieve are present, they can impede the manifestation process. These feelings of stress, impatience, and overwhelm often arise from fear and can distract you from your goals. Stop focusing on the how and the tasks at hand and focus on your end goal. Yes, it is that simple. By finding joy and pleasure in envisioning the manifestation of your future goals and maintaining focus on the end goal, you can overcome these obstacles and achieve success. Cultivating a positive mindset, embracing happiness, and maintaining a cheerful demeanor are essential. Doing so allows you to navigate your tasks smoothly, and your goals will manifest sooner than anticipated. So, keep smiling, stay positive, and believe in the power of your dreams.

Visualization is a mental technique where you construct clear mental images or scenarios of your desired goals or outcomes. It involves using your imagination to visualize, feel, and immerse yourself in these goals as if they've already become a reality. Visualization taps into the power of your thoughts and emotions to create a mental blueprint of your goals and aspirations. By regularly visualizing your goals, you work on aligning your subconscious mind with your intentions, making your desires seem more achievable and tangible. By vividly experiencing your goals as if they have already been achieved, you infuse them with a sense of reality and possibility. It's a practice aimed at boosting your confidence in your ability to accomplish your goals and maintaining a positive outlook. With each visualization session, you cultivate a positive mindset that propels you forward, even in adversity.

In simpler terms, think of visualization as a specific tool within the more significant practice of manifesting. It's the process of crafting mental images or scenarios to reinforce your belief and concentration while manifesting encompasses the complete journey of attracting and materializing your goals into real-life experiences through a combination of mental and practical actions.

Manifesting and visualization are powerful techniques that allow you to tap into the limitless potential of your mind. By envisioning your desired outcomes and immersing yourselves in the associated emotions, you create a magnetic force that draws these experiences into your life. This is where the Law of Attraction comes into play.

The Law of Attraction states that like attracts like. It suggests that the energy you emit through your thoughts, emotions, and beliefs attracts corresponding experiences and circumstances. When you align your thoughts and emotions with the positive outcomes you desire, you send out a vibrational frequency that resonates with those experiences. In the context of manifesting and visualization, the Law of Attraction reminds you of the importance of maintaining a positive mindset and unwavering belief in your ability to manifest your desires. It encourages you to focus on what you want rather than what you lack, as your attention and energy shape your reality. Ask, believe, receive.

By incorporating the Law of Attraction into your manifesting and visualization practices, you consciously choose to attract abundance, success, and joy into your life. You become a deliberate creator of your reality, understanding that your thoughts and emotions are powerful magnets that draw in your desired experiences.

ACTION ITEMS:

Manifesting is a practice that requires consistency, belief, and alignment of your thoughts, emotions, beliefs, and actions. By following these action items, you can begin to harness the power of manifestation and bring your dreams into reality.

- **Set Clear Intentions:** Clearly define what you want to manifest. Be specific about the details and visualize your desired outcome.
- **Visualize with Emotion:** Create vibrant mental images of your goals as if they have already been achieved. Engage your senses and feel the emotions associated with your success.
- **Align Your Beliefs:** Identify and challenge any limiting beliefs hindering your manifestation. Replace them with empowering beliefs that support your goals.
- **Take Inspired Action:** Actively pursue opportunities and take steps towards your desired outcome. Trust your intuition and follow through with inspired actions that align with your intentions.
- **Practice Gratitude:** Cultivate an attitude of gratitude for what you already have and for the manifestation that is on its way. Express gratitude daily and appreciate the progress you make along the journey.

SUMMARY

Manifesting and visualization are transformative practices that enable you to manifest your desires and goals intentionally. By setting clear intentions and vividly visualizing your desired outcomes, you align your thoughts, emotions, and energy with what you want to attract. The Law of Attraction emphasizes that your thoughts and emotions emit a vibrational frequency that draws corresponding experiences and circumstances into your life. Maintaining a positive mindset, self-belief, and taking inspired actions are crucial to succeed in manifestation.

WE CAN MANIFEST SMALL OR BIG THINGS

It was a familiar melody, one that had resonated with my soul for the past couple of days. Yet, I couldn't name the song or recall the artist behind it. I cherished that tune, but it remained as a vague, elusive hum in my mind. Perhaps you've experienced that feeling too, the yearning to know something so desperately, yet it eludes your grasp.

The melody lingered within me until I made a firm declaration: I was determined to uncover its identity. Two days later, at the break of dawn, I set out on my morning run. As I turned a corner, my eyes fell upon an elderly gentleman with his vintage BMW parked in the driveway. He was washing his car this early in the morning, adding charm to the moment. An ancient radio player was on the side of his house, perched on a small wall. And as I drew nearer, the lyrics of the elusive song filled the air.

A smile spread across my face, and I marveled at the peculiar scene unfolding before me at 7 a.m. My heart brimmed with joy. It reminded us that sometimes, life presents us with the answers we seek in the most unexpected ways."

"POSITIVE AFFIRMATIONS
ARE THE BEGINNING STEPS
TO RESHAPING YOUR THINKING
AND ULTIMATELY YOUR LIFE."

BRYANT MCGILL

CHAPTER 19

AFFIRMATIONS AND INCANTATIONS

Affirmations are positive statements or declarations that you can use to reinforce and reprogram your thoughts, beliefs, and attitudes. They are powerful tools for self-improvement. Repeating affirmations regularly can shift your mindset, boost your confidence, and attract positive outcomes into your life.

The practice of employing affirmations has its origins in ancient Egyptian and Greek cultures. Over the centuries, this practice has evolved within different cultures and philosophical traditions. Affirmations gained significant traction in the early 20th century, particularly within the New Thought movement. Notably, author Emile Coué crafted the famous affirmation, "Every day, in every way, I am getting better and better," which has been embraced and adapted by many motivational speakers and life coaches.

Affirmations should be written down in the present tense as if your desired outcome has already been achieved. They are designed to counteract your negative self-talk and replace it with empowering and uplifting thoughts. Emphasizing the importance of framing your affirmations positively is crucial. When crafting your affirmations, using language that expresses your desires rather than dwelling on what you wish to avoid is essential. This is because the Universe responds to the energy and intentions you emit.

When you construct your affirmations with positive language, you channel your thoughts and emotions toward attracting what you want in life instead of what you do not want. For instance, instead of saying, "I don't want to be sick," it is important to phrase it as "I want to be healthy." Or instead of saying, "I am not good enough," a new affirmation could be, "I am confident and capable in all that I do." This shift in language fosters a more positive mindset, which will draw your desired outcomes and opportunities toward you.

It's vital to genuinely believe in the affirmative statements and connect with the emotions they carry. By consistently and confidently repeating affirmations, you can reshape your subconscious mind and harmonize your thoughts with your desired reality. This process elevates your energetic state and your vibration, thus putting you in a receptive mode to manifest your goals.

Affirmations can be used in various areas of life, such as self-esteem, health, relationships, career, and abundance. They can be written down, spoken aloud, or even visualized. The key is choosing affirmations that resonate with you personally and reflect the positive changes you wish to manifest.

ACTION ITEMS:

Read over the affirmations and see which ones resonate with your energy level. You can adopt them or change them to your liking. (More affirmations can be found at the end of this book) Grab your journal and record the affirmations that resonate most with you. Consider jotting them on a small notecard that you can keep in your purse, wallet, or car. This way, you'll have a handy reference while on the go until the affirmations become second nature. Experiment with these affirmations for various aspects of your life, and if they don't quite fit, don't hesitate to personalize them to better suit your needs.

Self-esteem and Confidence:

- I am worthy of love and respect just as I am.
- I embrace my unique qualities and celebrate my individuality.
- I radiate self-confidence and attract positive opportunities.

Health and Well-being:

- I am grateful for my body and treat it with love and care.
- I am strong, vibrant, and full of energy.
- Every day, I am becoming healthier and more balanced.

Relationships and Connection:

- I attract loving and supportive relationships into my life.
- I am deserving of a healthy and fulfilling relationship.
- I am surrounded by positive and uplifting people who inspire me.

Career and Success:

- I am capable and deserving of success in my chosen career.
- I am focused and motivated, and I take consistent action towards my goals.
- I attract abundance and prosperity into my professional life.

Abundance and Prosperity:

- I am worthy of financial abundance and success.
- I am aligned with the energy of abundance and attract it effortlessly.
- I deserve to live a life of abundance and prosperity.

Weight loss:

- I control my food choices to support my weight loss.
- I am grateful that I am losing weight effortlessly.
- I am becoming healthier and stronger every day, in every way.

Money and Wealth:

- I live in abundance, and money flows to me quickly and effortlessly.
- I attract lucrative opportunities and financial blessings.
- I am a magnet for wealth and prosperity.
- I deserve financial freedom and the ability to live a life of abundance.

Stay Engaged:

- To keep your affirmations fresh and engaging, periodically introduce new ones into your practice. This prevents monotony and keeps your mind receptive to new possibilities. Experiment with affirmations that resonate with your current goals and aspirations.

Incantations

Similar to affirmations, you will use incantations to shift your mindset, boost confidence, and attract positive experiences. An incantation is a spoken or chanted formula of words believed to have magical or spiritual power, almost like a magic spell. It is often used in rituals, ceremonies, or spiritual practices to invoke a desired outcome or to connect with higher energies or entities. Incantations have been practiced spiritually by various cultures, religions, and belief systems throughout history.

For instance, Buddhism and Hinduism often use chanting and incantations, such as reciting mantras, as part of their meditation and spiritual practices. These mantras are believed to invoke blessings and wisdom. In Christianity, prayers and psalms can be seen as a form of incantation. Repeated recitation of certain prayers, like the Rosary, is believed to bring spiritual benefits. These practices lead to spiritual awakening and closeness to God or the Universe.

As you embark on your personal growth and mindset journey, consider harnessing the power of incantations. Here's a simple guide on how to employ them effectively:

- Find a comfortable place to sit, and set a timer for a brief period, ideally between 3 to 5 minutes.
- Repeatedly chant your chosen uplifting and empowering incantation, infusing it with unwavering belief and intention.

Why is this practice beneficial? It serves as a means to rewire your subconscious mind, harmonizing your thoughts and beliefs with your aspirations and goals.

Just like affirmations, incantations are your go-to tools for changing your mindset, supercharging your confidence, and pulling in those positive vibes. When you chant or recite specific words or phrases, you support your positive beliefs, ditch the limiting ones, and create this mega-energy that fuels your goals and dreams. But remember, the magic happens when you bring your belief and intent to the game. Your energy and focus are the secret sauce that makes it all work.

In the end, whether you're all about affirmations or diving into incantations, the goal is the same: use the power of words and thoughts to make your life unique and get those goals within reach. It's all about you taking the reins of your own destiny!

Here are some short incantations that you can use for various purposes:

- "I am powerful, strong."
- "I deserve love, success, and abundance."
- "I am a magnet for positive opportunities."

ACTION ITEMS:

- Retrieve your journal and craft five affirmations you commit to using daily for the next 30 days. Try to make them as short as possible so you can easily repeat them over and over again. Whether you're out for a jog with your furry friend, taking a stroll in nature, or even driving in your car, use these affirmations to keep your thoughts focused and positive.
- Write down your personal incantations. And remember, the power of incantations lies in repetition, intention, and belief. Choose the incantations that resonate with you the most or create your own, and repeat them over and over again for 3-5 minutes with conviction and positivity. Allow the words to sink into your subconscious mind and align with your mindset. Do this daily.

SUMMARY

Affirmations and incantations are ancient practices. They transform your mindset, boost confidence, and attract positive outcomes. Frame affirmations positively, aligning thoughts with desires. Repeat them to reshape your subconscious and raise your vibration for manifestation. Use them in various life areas. Similar to mantras in spirituality, incantations connect you with higher energies for desired outcomes, encouraging personal growth and positive self-talk.

SAMPLE MORNING GRATITUDE

Each day, during my Happy Power Hour, I embark on a run. While jogging, I engage in a practice of repeating incantations and gratitude. I tailor the content to suit the day, investing a minimum of 30 minutes in this ritual. Occasionally, distractions disrupt my thoughts, but I redirect my focus as soon as I notice. I employ concise incantations repeatedly, embedding them in my subconscious mind.

Thank you, thank you, thank you for my healthy body. Thank you for my healthy knees and the ability to run. Thank you for my healthy heart and my healthy spine, allowing me to run upright. Thank you for my upcoming Bali vacation (this is a future gratitude). Thank you for the amazing beaches in Bali and the wonderful people I meet there; thank you for the fun I have. Thank you for my fantastic hotel, and thank you for the smooth travel. Thanks for the beautiful weather. Thank you for my home, thank you for my comfortable bed, thank you for the food in my fridge. Thank you for the convenience of being able to go to the grocery store and shop for what I need. Thanks for my daughter; I'm thankful for her happiness, and thank you for my daughter's good health. Thank you to all my friends, and thank you to my family. Thank you for the enjoyable dinner party I had last night. Thank you for the laughter we shared. Thank you for the abundance in my life; thank you that I live in abundance. Thank you that I am safe. Thank you that I am loved. Thank you for my strengths. Thank you for all the abundance around me. Thank you for my happiness. Thank you that I am safe. Thank you for having arrived. Thank you for my fun life. Thank you for the abundance.

PART THREE

GOOD KARMA AND GIVING BACK

"SYNCHRONICITY IS A WINK
FROM THE UNIVERSE, A NOD
FROM THE DIVINE, REMINDING
US THAT WE ARE CONNECTED
TO SOMETHING GREATER
THAN OURSELVES."

GABRIELLE BERNSTEIN

CHAPTER 20

SYNCHRONICITIES

On your path toward manifesting your desires, you will encounter many synchronicities. They can be seen as meaningful coincidences or events that seem to be perfectly aligned with your intentions. These occurrences may appear as if they were orchestrated by the Universe, bringing together people, opportunities, or circumstances that align with your thoughts, emotions, and beliefs. Synchronicities are a sign of the interconnectedness of the Universe.

When you engage in practices such as affirmations, visualizations, and manifesting, you are actively directing your focus and energy toward your desired outcomes. Thoughts become things, and synchronicities can be seen as signs or confirmations that you are on the right path and in alignment with your intentions. They serve as reminders that the Universe is responding to your thoughts and emotions, bringing forth experiences that resonate with your desires. Welcome synchronicities with a joyful smile and bask in the delight they bring.

Synchronicities can manifest in various ways. For example, you may have a specific intention or desire in mind, and suddenly, you come across a book, a conversation, or an unexpected opportunity that directly relates to what you were seeking. It may feel like a meaningful coincidence or a serendipitous event that aligns perfectly with your thoughts and desires.

In the context of karma, synchronicities reflect the energy you put into the world. Positive actions and intentions will attract positive synchronicities, while negative actions and intentions lead to challenging or unfavorable synchronicities. The energy you emit through your thoughts, emotions, and actions influences the synchronicities that come into your life.

It's important to note that synchronicities are not mere coincidences but rather meaningful occurrences that hold significance for you personally. They serve as reminders to stay aligned with your desires, to trust the process, and to continue practicing the techniques that support your manifestation journey.

Embracing synchronicities involves being open and aware of the signs and opportunities that come your way. Pay attention to the patterns, connections, and coincidences that align with your intentions. By acknowledging and appreciating these synchronicities, you strengthen your belief in the power of manifestation and the interconnectedness of the Universe. As you journey further, you come to understand that synchronicities are the Universe's way of communicating with you. They are its nod of approval. With every synchronicity, the Universe gently reminds you that you are the co-creator of your reality and that your dreams are worth pursuing with courage and conviction. By recognizing and embracing these meaningful coincidences, you can gain insights, make connections, and align yourself with the flow of abundance in your life.

ACTION ITEMS:

These action items are meant to help you deepen your understanding and engagement with synchronicities.

- **Cultivate Awareness:** Develop a heightened sense of awareness in your daily life. Pay attention to subtle signs, coincidences, and connections around you. Practice mindfulness to observe and reflect on these experiences.

- **Your Journal:** Dedicate a section of your journal for recording meaningful coincidences, signs, or events that align with your desires. Reflect on the emotions, thoughts, or actions that may have preceded these synchronicities.
- **Follow Inspired Action:** Trust your intuition and take inspired action when synchronicities occur. Embrace opportunities that align with your desires and move forward with confidence.
- **Embrace the Power of Trust:** Recognize that synchronicities are profound signs from the Universe. Use them as reminders to trust and believe even more in the manifestation process. Remember the mantra "Ask, Believe, Receive" and let it guide your mindset and actions. Trust that the Universe is working in your favor and that these synchronicities are guiding you toward the fulfillment of your desires.

SUMMARY

Synchronicities are meaningful coincidences that align with your intentions to manifest your desires. They signify the interconnectedness of the Universe and can appear as if orchestrated by it. By practicing manifestation techniques, you direct your focus and energy, and synchronicities serve as signs that you're on the right path. They reflect the Universe responding to your thoughts and emotions, encouraging you to trust the process and continue your manifestation journey.

GOOD-BYE ANXIETY

From my twenties through my late forties, I grappled with anxiety attacks or panic episodes, which would unpredictably strike me from time to time. They often occurred when I was driving alone in my car, particularly when caught in traffic jams. These episodes manifested with severe symptoms, including a racing heart, chest discomfort, tingling sensations in my lips and fingers, and dizziness.

My attempts to alleviate these attacks through music or opening windows proved futile. When stuck on a congested highway, I would desperately seek an escape route, scanning for the nearest exit or contemplating abandoning my car and walking home. At times, I reached out to friends for assistance, while on other occasions, I simply parked my car and departed.

In hindsight, I now realize that these panic attacks served as metaphors for my life. They occurred during periods when I felt trapped or was living a life incongruent with my true values and desires. This included staying in unfulfilling relationships and enduring financial, emotional, and workplace exploitation, all of which left me drained. Unfortunately, at the time, I remained oblivious to this connection.

It wasn't until I uncovered the profound meaning behind the phrase "It's your choice to be happy!" that I recognized how much power I had given to fear. For years, I had engaged in a constant battle with my fears, immersing myself in them during therapy sessions and continuous self-talk, unwittingly magnifying their influence.

Only when I encountered the tools presented in this book did I begin to regain control over my life. I had allowed panic attacks to dominate my existence, unaware that my body, mind, and soul were attempting to communicate with me, highlighting areas requiring my attention.

For instance, the last panic attack I experienced happened a couple of years ago while I was in a two-year relationship with a man who, unfortunately, was not the right person for me. One day, as I drove through heavy city traffic, an anxiety attack crept up on me. However, by then, I had already acquired the knowledge I'm sharing in this book. I recognized the onset of the attack, with my heart racing. Instead of succumbing to it, I mentally raised a stop sign and began reciting my gratitude list, redirecting my focus immediately to more pleasant topics.

As soon as the opportunity arose, I pulled into a parking lot, not to combat the attack but to acknowledge it. I conversed with my fear as if it were an old friend, saying, "I see you. I understand something is amiss, and I promise to investigate it." I relaxed, employed my breathing techniques, focused on the positives in my life, put on a smile, and swiftly brought the attack under control.

In the following days, I delved deep into my journal, asking probing questions about my relationship, assessing why I was staying, and whether my needs were being met. It didn't take long to realize that I was far from happy and that my relationship was built on an illusion. Consequently, I promptly ended the relationship and dedicated myself to my daily transformation routine. I had faith in what I was doing and was able to let go.

I consistently wore a smile regularly tuned into my "Happy State," even in the midst of the breakup and the accompanying sadness. I found solace in dancing to uplifting music and repeated my affirmations throughout the day, whether I was driving, working out, or shopping. I remained resilient. Not only did I successfully conclude a two-year relationship that had held a significant emotional investment, but I also navigated the demanding phase of the breakup, financial challenges, the quest for a new place to live, and the defense of my decision without succumbing to anxiety. During the move, my former partner lightheartedly commented, "I don't know how you do it, but you're like a breakup role model."

I improved my overall well-being by taking care of my body, sticking to a regular fitness routine, practicing meditation, engaging in enjoyable activities, traveling, and participating in various events and workshops. Before embarking on my search for a new home, I not only listed my preferences but also visualized them. Shortly afterward, a series of synchronicities began to unfold, serving as a reassuring sign from the Universe to trust the process and stay aligned with my desires. These synchronicities brought extraordinary individuals and opportunities into my life, demonstrating the effectiveness of the Law of Attraction. Upon settling into my new residence, I realized that I was happier than I had ever been during that relationship. I had nurtured self-love, embraced my inner strength, and the feeling was profoundly exhilarating.

"THE SIMPLEST
THINGS ARE OFTEN
THE TRUEST."

RICHARD BACH

CHAPTER 21

EASY IS RIGHT AND RIGHT IS EASY

In the grand journey of life, you'll discover a beautiful truth: when you walk the path of moral integrity aligned with your values, life becomes a symphony of simplicity. A gentle ease permeates your existence, a lightness that uplifts your spirit. You become unburdened, more detached, and at peace with your fellow beings and the world around you. In this realm of ease, work becomes joyful and fun, and relationships bloom effortlessly. Your positivity becomes a radiant force, touching everything that crosses your path.

Along your way, challenges will come, but when faced with choices, you'll notice the magic of simplicity at play. Your newfound happiness and alignment enable you to connect with your intuition effortlessly. Your gut feelings become a trusted guide, and decisions flow with grace. Repeat this affirmation along your journey: "Easy is right, and right is easy." Step back and choose the simplest, most right path when life's complexities cloud your way. This wisdom applies to both your professional and personal realms. Avoid needless complications and sidestep strenuous situations. Remember, the right path is always the easiest.

In the spirit of Deepak Chopra, who explored this essence in the "Law of Least Effort," embrace the art of flowing with the natural order. Resist the urge to overthink or complicate. When you align with the right path and make morally sound choices, life becomes a gentle breeze. The virtuous way should always feel like the most effortless path, a beacon lighting your way.

When your goals harmonize with your values, something remarkable unfolds. The work required feels lighter, infused with purpose, and surrounded by positive karma. Intrinsically right endeavors tend to flow smoother. Embrace this flow into your life - reducing stress and friction.

The journey toward your goals and desires may still hold challenges and tests of your resolve, yet it all feels easier. Driven by your authenticity and sense of what's right, you meet obstacles with resilience. The work remains demanding but aligns effortlessly with your values, making it feel not just right but easy. You're not merely pursuing success but cultivating positive karma as you progress. This positivity attracts opportunities and fosters a sense of ease in your life.

So, as you embrace the mantra "Easy is right and right is easy," life unfolds with grace and reward. You not only experience personal growth but also sow the seeds of positive karma, enhancing your journey with boundless positivity. You embark on a purposeful and fulfilling voyage by aligning your goals with your values and choosing the easy and right path. Stay true to yourself, keep striving, and watch as the Universe responds in kind. Your journey becomes an epic tale of ease, grace, and profound fulfillment.

ACTION ITEMS:

- **Positive Mindset:** Dedicate time each day to focus on nurturing a positive mindset. Engage in activities that uplift your spirit, such as meditation, gratitude journaling, chanting positive affirmations, or reading inspirational books. The positivity starts from within, so make it a daily practice.

- **Practice Good Karma:** Be mindful of your actions and their impact on others. Strive to radiate positivity and kindness in your interactions. Small acts of goodwill, like helping someone in need or offering a sincere compliment, can create a ripple effect of positive karma.

- **Align with Your Values**: Reflect on your core values and beliefs. Ensure that your daily actions and decisions align with these values. When your choices are in harmony with your principles, life becomes more straightforward and authentic.
- **Embrace Simplicity**: Simplify your life by decluttering both your physical and mental spaces. Focus on the essentials, and let go of unnecessary complications. Prioritize tasks and relationships that bring joy and fulfillment.
- **Trust Your Intuition**: Practice tuning into your intuition and gut feelings. When faced with decisions, take a moment to connect with your inner wisdom. Trust that your intuition will guide you toward the most straightforward and most right choices.

Positivity affirmations:

- "I trust my intuition to guide me towards both easy and right choices."
- "Simplicity is my ally, and I embrace it in every aspect of my life."
- "Every day, I allow the natural flow of life to bring me peace, joy, and abundance."

SUMMARY

In life's journey, you'll discover that the easiest path often aligns with what is right, leading to simplicity and moral integrity. Embracing the mantra "Easy is right, and right is easy" empowers you to make choices that bring harmony and fulfillment in both personal and professional realms, creating a purposeful and gentle journey.

LOVE STRIKES BACK

Once upon a time, in the land of teenage turmoil, my 13-year-old daughter and I were locked in an epic battle of wills. Every encounter felt like a high-stakes showdown, and our disagreements were like fireworks on the Fourth of July. One fateful Thursday, things took a turn for the worse, with doors slamming and communication hitting rock bottom. Getting her to school every day was like walking a tightrope, and picking her up was no picnic either.

On Saturday morning, I trudged into the kitchen, already bracing myself for another round of teenage drama. We met in the kitchen, and the inevitable clash began. This time, it all started with a debate about milk. I stormed out of the house, seeking refuge beneath my beloved palm tree to gather my thoughts.

As I sat there pondering how to mend our fractured relationship, I decided to call upon the Universe for help. Miraculously, within five minutes, a revelation struck me like lightning: "Kill the situation with love."

With a grin spreading across my face, I envisioned a plan. If I showered her with compliments, compassion, and boundless love, maybe, just maybe, I could turn the tide. I recalled the teachings of the Dalai Lama, who emphasized the power of love and compassion to heal any situation.

Upon my return, my daughter was still in the kitchen. I couldn't resist, so I complimented her outfit ever so briefly. Silence followed, and she retreated to her room.

Throughout the day, I maintained my newfound attitude of happiness. Whenever our paths crossed, I refused to engage in arguments, opting instead for heartfelt declarations of love and encouragement. Eventually, she left for a friend's house.

When she returned that evening, I greeted her with genuine warmth and another compliment, thanking her for being punctual. She headed upstairs to her room, but an hour later, she made a surprise appearance on the stairs.

"Mom, what's going on?" she asked, her curiosity piqued. "You've been nothing but nice to me all day, even when I was being difficult."

With a loving smile, I replied, "Well, it's simple. I really love you, and it's perfectly okay if we don't always see eye to eye. How about some popcorn and a movie?"

She burst into laughter, and just like that, the three-day standoff that had gripped our household was conquered by the power of LOVE.

"HOW PEOPLE TREAT YOU
IS THEIR KARMA;
HOW YOU REACT
IS YOURS."

WAYNE DYERYOU

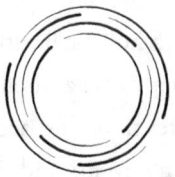

CHAPTER 22

KARMA OR CAUSE AND EFFECT

Have you ever noticed that when you extend kindness to others, it feels like the Universe responds with a smile? Karma is often described as a bit like the Universe's way of balancing things out. It is a concept originating from Hinduism, Buddhism, and Jainism that says the things you do, the thoughts you think, and even your intentions have a way of coming back to you.

If you put out positivity and do good deeds, you are planting seeds for good things to happen to you now and in the future. But, on the flip side, if you do negative things or you engage in harmful activity, these actions can come back to you, too. It's like a cosmic balance sheet where your actions have consequences, whether it's in this life or maybe in a future one, depending on what you believe.

The concept of cause and effect is used in science and philosophy, which actually complements Karma. Both concepts revolve around the principle that what you do or intend to do directly impacts what happens in your life and the world around you. Cause and effect asserts that every action or event has a cause or multiple causes, which in turn lead to specific effects or outcomes. Cause and effect reminds you that actions have results, and everything is connected in this big web of life.

Deepak Chopra, a renowned author, speaker, and alternative medicine advocate known for his work in holistic health, spirituality, and mind-body wellness, often emphasizes that cause and effect are interconnected in our lives. He suggests that our intentions and actions create ripples in the Universe, influencing the following events and circumstances. He encourages a mindful approach to our choices, as they can have far-reaching consequences, both for ourselves and the world around us.

As you can see, it is important for you to take responsibility for your actions and understand their potential impact on your overall well-being and the world at large.

So, whether you're thinking about karma or cause and effect, the main message is similar: the things you do matter and have consequences. If you put out positivity and do good, it will come back to you in some way. However, it's important to note that if we engage in unkindness or make poor choices, the consequences of our actions can also find their way back to us. It's a reminder that you have a role in shaping your life, and it's up to you to make choices that lead to the outcomes you want.

The familiar saying goes, "You reap what you sow." If you want to foster happiness into your life and strive for personal growth, then you must become skilled at planting the seeds of joy and doing good deeds. In simpler terms, when you intentionally make choices that promote happiness and success for both yourself and others, the result, in the realm of karma, is the manifestation of happiness and success.

ACTION ITEMS:

Empower yourself by making conscious choices and taking actions that radiate goodwill, kindness, and positive energy in your life and the lives of others. Each action you take has the power to create a positive impact. Practicing positive karma is an ongoing journey that often starts with small, everyday actions. Over time, these actions accumulate and shape your overall karmic energy, influencing the experiences and opportunities that come your way.

- **Embrace the power of gratitude:** Start each day by expressing gratitude for the blessings in your life, not only for what you have but also for the people who enrich your life. Gratitude breeds positivity and attracts more abundance.
- **Random acts of kindness:** Make it a mission to spread kindness wherever you go. Small gestures like holding the door for someone, helping a stranger in need, or buying a coffee for the person behind you in line can create a ripple effect of positivity and can have a big effect on others.
- **Forgive and let go:** Holding onto grudges and resentment creates negative energy. Practice forgiveness, not just for others but also for yourself. Letting go of the past frees you to create positive experiences in the present.
- **Harness the power of positive thoughts and words:** Be mindful of your thoughts and words. Replace self-doubt with empowering affirmations and speak kindly to yourself and others.
- **Cultivate empathy:** Develop a deep understanding and connection with others by practicing empathy. Put yourself in their shoes and offer support and compassion. This empathy will lead to more compassionate actions and interactions.
- **Prioritize self-care:** Take care of yourself physically, mentally, and emotionally. Prioritize self-care activities that recharge and rejuvenate you, enabling you to radiate positivity.
- **Support others' dreams:** Be a cheerleader for others' aspirations. Celebrate their successes, offer encouragement, and lend a helping hand. Together, we can achieve greatness.
- **Give without expecting anything in return:** When you give your time, resources, or assistance to others, do it selflessly. Don't expect

recognition or repayment; instead, find joy in the act of giving itself.

- **Reduce harm to the environment:** Be conscious of your impact on the environment. Adopt sustainable practices, reduce waste, and contribute to the well-being of our planet. This way, you will contribute to positive karma on a larger scale.
- **Master the art of active listening:** Engage in meaningful conversations by practicing active listening. Show genuine interest, offer support, and create a positive space for connection.
- **Practice patience:** In challenging situations, exercise patience and understanding. Reacting with anger or frustration can create negative karma.
- **Lead with inspiration:** Be a shining example of positivity and empowerment. Lead by example, inspire others through your actions, and create a ripple effect of positive change.
- **Be honest and transparent:** Honesty builds trust, and transparency in your actions and communications creates positive karma. Be truthful and ethical in your dealings with others.
- **Avoid harmful habits:** Refrain from actions that harm yourself or others, such as lying, cheating, or engaging in destructive behaviors.
- **Educate yourself:** Continuously learn about different cultures, beliefs, and perspectives. This knowledge can help you become more open-minded and inclusive in your actions.
- **Volunteer and support causes:** Contribute your time and resources to charitable organizations or causes you believe in. This not only helps those in need but also brings a sense of fulfillment and positive karma into your life.

SUMMARY

Karma is the universal law of cause and effect. It teaches that your actions, thoughts, and intentions create a cosmic balance sheet. Good deeds lead to positive outcomes, while negative actions have consequences. This concept aligns with cause and effect, emphasizing the interconnectedness of all actions and their impact on well-being and the world. Karma reminds us that our choices shape our lives and the world around us, encouraging us to cultivate positivity and good deeds for a brighter future.

KARMA AND THE LAW OF ATTRACTION

Karma and the Law of Attraction share a common thread in their understanding of cause and effect. Both concepts recognize that our thoughts, actions, and intentions have consequences that reverberate back to us. Karma, rooted in various spiritual traditions, suggests that our actions create energetic imprints that shape our future experiences. Similarly, the Law of Attraction posits that we magnetically attract what we focus on and visualize into our lives.

By aligning our thoughts, emotions, and intentions with our desired outcomes, we draw those experiences closer to us. Both Karma and the Law of Attraction emphasize the power of conscious intention and the understanding that our energetic vibrations influence the reality we manifest. By cultivating positive thoughts, embodying kindness, and visualizing our desired outcomes, we can actively participate in shaping our destiny and attracting the experiences we seek.

"THE BEST WAY TO FIND
YOURSELF IS TO LOSE
YOURSELF IN THE
SERVICE OF OTHERS."

MAHATMA GANDHI

CHAPTER 23

GIVING BACK AND CONTRIBUTION

Giving back and contributing is like spreading good karma and lending a hand to make the world a better place. It's all about sharing what you've got and helping out with things that are bigger than just you. Picture it as a gust of wind stirring a field of dandelions – the seeds scatter, touching individuals, communities, and the global landscape.

You can give your time and money or share your skills and resources. It's about you helping those who need a hand and supporting projects that bring positivity. With your newfound positive mindset, this should come naturally to you. But it's more than just doing charity; it's about getting involved and making a lasting impact.

Contribution is all about those little acts of kindness, the hours spent volunteering, the wisdom shared, and the talents you put out there for others. You know that we're all connected, and the good you do will set off a chain reaction of more good in the world.

When you give back and contribute, you're not only changing other people's lives – you're also being a total inspiration to those around you. It's like finding a bigger purpose and adding a dose of positivity and unity to your own life.

These good vibes can happen on a big scale or in everyday gestures, whether you're helping out your local community, standing up for justice, or being a friend to the planet. The real deal is the intention behind your actions, spreading positivity no matter how big or small.

Contributing to others' well-being and the greater good isn't just good for them; it's a boost for you too. You grow, feel thankful, and get that warm and fuzzy feeling inside. It's a reminder that everything is connected, and we're all part of making the world better, and together, we can light up a brighter path for everyone.

Even your tiniest contribution can be like a spark that sets off some amazing changes. It's a reminder that together, we can make the world a better place filled with kindness, support, and shared dreams. So keep spreading those good vibes!

ACTION ITEMS:

Empower yourself to make a positive impact in your community and beyond:

- **Serve at a Local Soup Kitchen:** Step up to volunteer at a local soup kitchen, nourishing those in need with warmth and nourishment.
- **Share Your Resources:** Donate clothes, food, or other essentials to a homeless shelter or charity, providing vital support to those less fortunate.
- **Be a Mentor and Guide:** Offer your wisdom and guidance to a young person or someone seeking support, empowering them on their journey.
- **Champion the Environment:** Join community clean-up events, actively preserving and maintaining the environment for future generations.
- **Raise Awareness and Funds:** Organize charity fundraisers, shining a light on important causes and generating resources to make

a difference.

- **Offer Your Professional Skills:** Utilize your expertise to provide pro bono services, enriching the lives of individuals and organizations in need.
- **Donate Blood, Save Lives:** Become a life-saving hero by donating blood to a blood bank, offering the gift of life to those in critical need.
- **Contribute to Conservation:** Plant trees and engage in reforestation efforts, playing a role in environmental conservation and sustainability.
- **Support Local Artisans:** Champion local businesses and artisans by purchasing their products and services, bolstering your community's vibrancy.
- **Lend a Caring Ear:** Be a compassionate listener, offering emotional support to those navigating challenging times.
- **Spread Kindness:** Make someone's day brighter by buying a cup of coffee for the person behind you or providing a meal to a homeless individual in front of a store.

SUMMARY

Giving back and contributing means spreading positivity and making the world better. It involves sharing your time, money, skills, and resources to help others and support positive projects. Whether it's a small act of kindness or a big-scale effort, your intention to spread positivity can inspire change and unity, benefiting both others and yourself. Together, we can create a brighter and kinder world.

A HELPING HAND

When you find yourself living a life of happiness, fulfillment, and abundance, a natural inclination arises within you to give back. Experiencing the joy and contentment that come from living in abundance opens your heart to the desire to help others and share your blessings. You recognize the interconnectedness of all beings and understand that by extending a helping hand, you contribute to the collective well-being. Giving back becomes a way to express gratitude for the abundance you have received and to make a positive impact in the lives of others. Whether it's through acts of kindness, sharing your resources, or using your skills to uplift others, the desire to give back becomes an integral part of your journey. It brings a deeper sense of purpose and fulfillment, knowing that you are making a difference and spreading happiness to those around you.

"WHAT YOU THINK
YOU BECOME.

WHAT YOU FEEL
YOU ATTRACT.

WHAT YOU IMAGINE
YOU CREATE."

BUDDHA

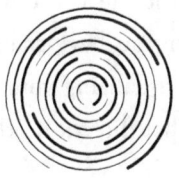

CHAPTER 24

THE 10 DAY POSITIVE MINDSET TRANSFORMATION

Take your journal and get ready to embark on a truly transformative journey. Once you've delved into Part 1 and Part 2 of this book, it's time to take action. Make sure to set aside dedicated time to complete the action items in each chapter that truly resonate with you. By taking these steps, you will establish a solid groundwork for your 10-day transformation and develop a deep comprehension of the importance of nurturing a positive mindset. This mindset will serve as the cornerstone for a life filled with joy, fulfillment, and abundance in all aspects.

During the upcoming ten days, make use of the Daily Transformation List and make a conscious effort to integrate the action items into your everyday regimen. Employ the Daily Checklist to track your progress as you successfully integrate each task into your daily routine. Cultivate a daily habit of reviewing your journal entries, observing your progress, and identifying areas to prioritize moving forward.

To establish a solid foundation for your new daily routine, take the time to fill in the blanks. As you've learned in Part 2 of this book, what you consistently think about throughout the day manifests in your reality.

Your energy follows your focus. Therefore, having clarity about your goals will empower you to create the life you desire. Keep in mind that every thought, belief, and emotion you have shaped your life. By consciously directing your thoughts and visualizing your desired outcomes, you guide your subconscious mind in that direction. The law of attraction will then work its magic.

Before diving into your daily routine, begin by writing down your top 3 goals in the provided list. Be exceptionally specific and ask yourself why you want to achieve these goals and how you will know when they are accomplished. Take the time to craft positive affirmations and incantations that resonate with you, which you will utilize over the next ten days. You can always modify them as needed, and if you need more suggestions, you will find additional affirmations at the end of this book. These affirmations will serve as a powerful tool to counteract negative self-talk throughout the day. Whenever a negative thought arises, visualize a stop sign in your mind and immediately recite your positive affirmations.

Next, document your limiting beliefs and substitute them with empowering ones in the provided list. You may discover additional limiting beliefs each day, and you have the ability to replace them as well. Whenever you catch yourself reciting a limiting belief in your mind, swiftly replace it with the empowering belief you have crafted.

Approach this transformation with enthusiasm, as these actions not only bring enjoyment but also cultivate happiness. Practice patience, forgiveness, and self-love, even if you happen to miss some action items throughout the day, understanding that you are giving your best effort. Your transformation is not a challenge or competition. It's about enriching your life, establishing a positive mindset, and nurturing happiness and fulfillment in the present and future. In just ten days, you will feel like a rejuvenated individual, experiencing profound joy in the present moment and laying the foundation for an extraordinary future

THE FOUNDATION FOR YOUR DAILY PRACTICE:

My top 3 Goals, (be specific):
_____
_____
_____
_____
_____

Why do I want to achieve these goals? (Be specific, because the clearer you get with your why the more motivated you will be).
_____
_____
_____
_____
_____
_____

My top 3 Positive Affirmations*:
_____
_____
_____
_____
_____

My top 3 Positive Incantations (the short ones)
_____
_____
_____

Old Limiting Belief   New Empowering Belief

_____
_____
_____
_____
_____

Sample affirmations can be found at the back of the book.

DAILY TRANSFORMATION LIST

Morning Routine:

- **Wake up Early:** Start your day by waking up an hour earlier, reserving this time exclusively for yourself.
- **Gratitude:** As you rise from bed, take a moment to reflect on the things you are grateful for. Express gratitude for each item until you reach the bathroom or your coffee maker. For further details, refer to Chapter 4.
- **The Happy Power Hour** (see chapter 10):
- **Cardiovascular Exercise:** Allocate the first 30 minutes to physical activity. Walk, run, swim, dance, practice yoga, or just jump around. During your workout, focus on affirmations or things you're grateful for, silently repeating them in your mind to empower your day.
- **Smile:** Following your workout, spend 2 minutes simply smiling.
- **Gratitude:** Set aside 10 minutes in a peaceful environment to reflect on what you're grateful for. Consider including your health, accomplishments, funny moments, friends and family, and exciting, romantic, and future moments.
- **Quiet Reflection:** Allocate 5 minutes to mindfulness or meditation.
- **Personal Development:** Dedicate 10-20 minutes to personal growth. Utilize your journal, work on affirmations of your beliefs, and establish your daily goals. Consider reading a book, watching motivational videos, or listening to audiobooks.
- **Visualization:** Reserve 5 minutes for visualizing your goals. Close your eyes and envision your future accomplishments and dreams coming true. Step into that vision, see, feel, and say "Thank You Universe," and smile. Let this feeling fill every cell of your body.

During The Day:

- **Your Journal:** Make it a daily habit to review your journal entries, observe your progress, and identify areas to focus on next.
- **Stay Hydrated:** Consume one full glass of water every 2 hours to maintain proper hydration throughout the day.
- **Nourish and Move:** Be mindful of your dietary choices during the day. Opt for stairs over elevators and aim to be more active. Create a list of changes you're willing to make in your diet and implement them. Include Superfoods in your daily diet.
- **Stop negative Self-talk:** Replace negative self-talk with positive affirmations.
- **Overcome Negative Thoughts and Limiting Beliefs:** Replace them with empowering thoughts and affirmations. Let go of old limited beliefs and embrace new empowering beliefs.
- **Your "Happy State:** When you need a quick power boost, enter your "Happy State." Remember, you can instantly influence three key elements: your physiology, your focus, and the language you use. For more details, consult chapter 6.
- **Just Smile:** Try to just smile three times per day, even if it feels forced, and maintain it for two minutes. By smiling, you activate the well-known happy hormones, creating a positive feedback loop in your body and mind.
- **Mindfulness Break:** Meditate or engage in mindfulness for 5-10 minutes daily.
- **Give Back:** Find a way to give back each day, whether it's a smile, a gift, a thank-you note, a hug, a supportive conversation, or a donation.
- **Goal Setting:** Review your top three goals and get to work. Stay laser-focused on where you want to go. When you feel overwhelmed with tasks, take a moment to reflect on the bigger picture. Envision the end result and what you want to achieve. Visualize what it would

look and feel like to attain your goals. For further information, refer to Chapter 15.

- **Take Action:** Engage in activities that align with your goals.
- **Daily Visualization:** Spend at least 5 minutes each day visualizing your goals. Close your eyes and envision your future accomplishments and dreams coming true. Step into that vision, see, feel, and say "Thank You Universe," and smile. Let this feeling fill every cell of your body.
- **Love yourself First:** Incorporate one activity into your daily routine that brings you joy and nourishes your well-being. This could include exercising, getting a massage, reading, taking a nap, spending time in nature, or meeting your best friends for coffee.

Evening Routine:

- **Priming Technique:** In the early evening, practice the priming technique. For more details, see Chapter 5.
- **Mindful Entertainment:** Choose mindful books or TV shows and limit your time on social media.
- **Synchronicities:** Take note of significant coincidences or events that occurred during the day, appearing to be in perfect alignment with your thoughts and desires. Regard them as validations from the Universe, indicating that you are on the right path. Refer to Chapter 21.
- **Bedtime Gratitude**: Before drifting into sleep, engage in a practice of gratitude. Include saying a "Thank You, Universe, that all of my dreams have come true"- this way, you are sending out the energetic vibration of receiving your goals.

DAILY CHECKLIST DAY 1

MORNING ROUTINE:

- [ ] Wake Up Early
- [ ] Gratitude while getting out of bed
- [ ] The "Happy Power Hour"
- [ ] Cardiovascular Exercise
- [ ] Smile after workout
- [ ] 10 min. Gratitude
- [ ] 5 min. Quiet Reflection
- [ ] Personal Development
- [ ] 5 Min. Visualization

DURING THE DAY:

- [ ] Stay Hydrated
- [ ] Nourish and Move
- [ ] Give Back
- [ ] Combat Negative Thoughts
- [ ] "HAPPY STATE"
- [ ] Just Smile 3 X
- [ ] 5 min Mindfulness Break
- [ ] Goal Setting
- [ ] Take Action towards your goals
- [ ] 5 min Daily Visualization
- [ ] Love yourself First

EVENING ROUTINE:

- [ ] Priming Technique
- [ ] Mindful Entertainment
- [ ] Synchronicities
- [ ] Bedtime Gratitude

DAILY CHECKLIST DAY 2

MORNING ROUTINE:
- ☐ Wake Up Early
- ☐ Gratitude while getting out of bed
- ☐ The "Happy Power Hour"
- ☐ Cardiovascular Exercise
- ☐ Smile after workout
- ☐ 10 min. Gratitude
- ☐ 5 min. Quiet Reflection
- ☐ Personal Development
- ☐ 5 Min. Visualization

DURING THE DAY:
- ☐ Stay Hydrated
- ☐ Nourish and Move
- ☐ Give Back
- ☐ Combat Negative Thoughts
- ☐ "HAPPY STATE"
- ☐ Just Smile 3 X
- ☐ 5 min Mindfulness Break
- ☐ Goal Setting
- ☐ Take Action towards your goals
- ☐ 5 min Daily Visualization
- ☐ Love yourself First

EVENING ROUTINE:
- ☐ Priming Technique
- ☐ Mindful Entertainment
- ☐ Synchronicities
- ☐ Bedtime Gratitude

DAILY CHECKLIST DAY 3

MORNING ROUTINE:

- [ ] Wake Up Early
- [ ] Gratitude while getting out of bed
- [ ] The "Happy Power Hour"
- [ ] Cardiovascular Exercise
- [ ] Smile after workout
- [ ] 10 min. Gratitude
- [ ] 5 min. Quiet Reflection
- [ ] Personal Development
- [ ] 5 Min. Visualization

DURING THE DAY:

- [ ] Stay Hydrated
- [ ] Nourish and Move
- [ ] Give Back
- [ ] Combat Negative Thoughts
- [ ] "HAPPY STATE"
- [ ] Just Smile 3 X
- [ ] 5 min Mindfulness Break
- [ ] Goal Setting
- [ ] Take Action towards your goals
- [ ] 5 min Daily Visualization
- [ ] Love yourself First

EVENING ROUTINE:

- [ ] Priming Technique
- [ ] Mindful Entertainment
- [ ] Synchronicities
- [ ] Bedtime Gratitude

DAILY CHECKLIST DAY 4

MORNING ROUTINE:

- [ ] Wake Up Early
- [ ] Gratitude while getting out of bed
- [ ] The "Happy Power Hour"
- [ ] Cardiovascular Exercise
- [ ] Smile after workout
- [ ] 10 min. Gratitude
- [ ] 5 min. Quiet Reflection
- [ ] Personal Development
- [ ] 5 Min. Visualization

DURING THE DAY:

- [ ] Stay Hydrated
- [ ] Nourish and Move
- [ ] Give Back
- [ ] Combat Negative Thoughts
- [ ] "HAPPY STATE"
- [ ] Just Smile 3 X
- [ ] 5 min Mindfulness Break
- [ ] Goal Setting
- [ ] Take Action towards your goals
- [ ] 5 min Daily Visualization
- [ ] Love yourself First

EVENING ROUTINE:

- [ ] Priming Technique
- [ ] Mindful Entertainment
- [ ] Synchronicities
- [ ] Bedtime Gratitude

DAILY CHECKLIST DAY 5

MORNING ROUTINE:

☐ Wake Up Early
☐ Gratitude while getting out of bed
☐ The "Happy Power Hour"
☐ Cardiovascular Exercise
☐ Smile after workout
☐ 10 min. Gratitude
☐ 5 min. Quiet Reflection
☐ Personal Development
☐ 5 Min. Visualization

DURING THE DAY:

☐ Stay Hydrated
☐ Nourish and Move
☐ Give Back
☐ Combat Negative Thoughts
☐ "HAPPY STATE"
☐ Just Smile 3 X
☐ 5 min Mindfulness Break
☐ Goal Setting
☐ Take Action towards your goals
☐ 5 min Daily Visualization
☐ Love yourself First

EVENING ROUTINE:

☐ Priming Technique
☐ Mindful Entertainment
☐ Synchronicities
☐ Bedtime Gratitude

DAILY CHECKLIST DAY 6

MORNING ROUTINE:

- [ ] Wake Up Early
- [ ] Gratitude while getting out of bed
- [ ] The "Happy Power Hour"
- [ ] Cardiovascular Exercise
- [ ] Smile after workout
- [ ] 10 min. Gratitude
- [ ] 5 min. Quiet Reflection
- [ ] Personal Development
- [ ] 5 Min. Visualization

DURING THE DAY:

- [ ] Stay Hydrated
- [ ] Nourish and Move
- [ ] Give Back
- [ ] Combat Negative Thoughts
- [ ] "HAPPY STATE"
- [ ] Just Smile 3 X
- [ ] 5 min Mindfulness Break
- [ ] Goal Setting
- [ ] Take Action towards your goals
- [ ] 5 min Daily Visualization
- [ ] Love yourself First

EVENING ROUTINE:

- [ ] Priming Technique
- [ ] Mindful Entertainment
- [ ] Synchronicities
- [ ] Bedtime Gratitude

DAILY CHECKLIST DAY 7

MORNING ROUTINE:

- [ ] Wake Up Early
- [ ] Gratitude while getting out of bed
- [ ] The "Happy Power Hour"
- [ ] Cardiovascular Exercise
- [ ] Smile after workout
- [ ] 10 min. Gratitude
- [ ] 5 min. Quiet Reflection
- [ ] Personal Development
- [ ] 5 Min. Visualization

DURING THE DAY:

- [ ] Stay Hydrated
- [ ] Nourish and Move
- [ ] Give Back
- [ ] Combat Negative Thoughts
- [ ] "HAPPY STATE"
- [ ] Just Smile 3 X
- [ ] 5 min Mindfulness Break
- [ ] Goal Setting
- [ ] Take Action towards your goals
- [ ] 5 min Daily Visualization
- [ ] Love yourself First

EVENING ROUTINE:

- [ ] Priming Technique
- [ ] Mindful Entertainment
- [ ] Synchronicities
- [ ] Bedtime Gratitude

DAILY CHECKLIST DAY 8

MORNING ROUTINE:

- [ ] Wake Up Early
- [ ] Gratitude while getting out of bed
- [ ] The "Happy Power Hour"
- [ ] Cardiovascular Exercise
- [ ] Smile after workout
- [ ] 10 min. Gratitude
- [ ] 5 min. Quiet Reflection
- [ ] Personal Development
- [ ] 5 Min. Visualization

DURING THE DAY:

- [ ] Stay Hydrated
- [ ] Nourish and Move
- [ ] Give Back
- [ ] Combat Negative Thoughts
- [ ] "HAPPY STATE"
- [ ] Just Smile 3 X
- [ ] 5 min Mindfulness Break
- [ ] Goal Setting
- [ ] Take Action towards your goals
- [ ] 5 min Daily Visualization
- [ ] Love yourself First

EVENING ROUTINE:

- [ ] Priming Technique
- [ ] Mindful Entertainment
- [ ] Synchronicities
- [ ] Bedtime Gratitude

DAILY CHECKLIST DAY 9

MORNING ROUTINE:

- [ ] Wake Up Early
- [ ] Gratitude while getting out of bed
- [ ] The "Happy Power Hour"
- [ ] Cardiovascular Exercise
- [ ] Smile after workout
- [ ] 10 min. Gratitude
- [ ] 5 min. Quiet Reflection
- [ ] Personal Development
- [ ] 5 Min. Visualization

DURING THE DAY:

- [ ] Stay Hydrated
- [ ] Nourish and Move
- [ ] Give Back
- [ ] Combat Negative Thoughts
- [ ] "HAPPY STATE"
- [ ] Just Smile 3 X
- [ ] 5 min Mindfulness Break
- [ ] Goal Setting
- [ ] Take Action towards your goals
- [ ] 5 min Daily Visualization
- [ ] Love yourself First

EVENING ROUTINE:

- [ ] Priming Technique
- [ ] Mindful Entertainment
- [ ] Synchronicities
- [ ] Bedtime Gratitude

DAILY CHECKLIST DAY 10

MORNING ROUTINE:

- ☐ Wake Up Early
- ☐ Gratitude while getting out of bed
- ☐ The "Happy Power Hour"
- ☐ Cardiovascular Exercise
- ☐ Smile after workout
- ☐ 10 min. Gratitude
- ☐ 5 min. Quiet Reflection
- ☐ Personal Development
- ☐ 5 Min. Visualization

DURING THE DAY:

- ☐ Stay Hydrated
- ☐ Nourish and Move
- ☐ Give Back
- ☐ Combat Negative Thoughts
- ☐ "HAPPY STATE"
- ☐ Just Smile 3 X
- ☐ 5 min Mindfulness Break
- ☐ Goal Setting
- ☐ Take Action towards your goals
- ☐ 5 min Daily Visualization
- ☐ Love yourself First

EVENING ROUTINE:

- ☐ Priming Technique
- ☐ Mindful Entertainment
- ☐ Synchronicities
- ☐ Bedtime Gratitude

SUGGESTED READING

Here is a list of some of my favorite books that have helped me create the toolkit for transforming your mindset and living a life of abundance, happiness, and joy. Please note that the books are listed in no particular order.

Shaolin *by Bernhard Moestl*
The Art of Happiness *by Dalai Lama and Howard Cutler*
Finding Inner Harmony *by Ralny Dann*
What I know for sure *by Oprah Winfrey*
The Art of Power *by Thich Nhat Hanh*
Embracing Your Inner Critic *by Hal Stone and Sidra Stone*
Notes from a Friend *by Tony Robbins*
Hero *by Rhonda Byrne*
The Book of Joy *by Dalai Lama and Archbishop Desmond Tutu*
The Secret *by Rhonda Byrne*
The Seven Spiritual Laws of Success *by Deepak Chopra*
Real Magic *by Dean Radin*
Young Forever *by Mark Hyman*
Radical Confidence *by Lisa Bilyen*
Connected to Goodness *by David Meltzer*
Think Like a Monk *by Jay Shetty*
Abundance *by Deepak Chopra*

Stop Missing Your Life *by Cory Muscara*
Habits of a Happy Brain *by Graziano Breuning*
Awareness *by Osho*
Unshakeable *by Tony Robbins*
The Power of Now *by Eckhart Tolle*
When the Shoe Fits *by Osho*
The Universe in a Single Atom *by Dalai Lama*
Giant Steps *by Tony Robbins*
Loving Kindness *by Sharon Salzberg*
Being Peace *by Thich Nhat Hanh*
Real Love *by Sharon Salzberg*
Peace is Every Step *by Thich Nhat Hanh*
You Can Create What You Want *by Jan Becker*
Crazy Sexy Diet *by Kris Carr*
Infinite Possibilities *by Mike Dooley*
Green for Life *by Don Colbert*
The Wisdom of Compassion *by Dalai Lama*
Unlimited Power *by Tony Robbins*
Path of Compassion *by Thich Nhat Hanh*
Beginning Mindfulness *by Andrew Weiss*
Manifesting Change *by Mike Dooley*
Start Where You Are *by Pema Chödrön*
The Wisdom of the Sands *by Bhagwan Shree Rajneesh*
Success and the Spirit *by Yogi Bhajan*
The Spell Book for New Witches *by Ambrosia Hawthorn*
The Food Babe Way *by Vani Hari*
Limitless *by Jim Kwik*
The China Study *by Thomas Campbell T. Colin Campbell*
Set Boundaries, Find Peace *by Nedra Glover Tawwab*
Atomic Habits *by James Clear*
The Power of Moments *by Dan Heath and Chip Heath*
How to Stop Worrying and Start Living *by Dale Carnegie*
The Happiness Project *by Gretchen Rubin*
Mindfulness *by Olivia Telford*
The Mountain *by Is You Brianna Wiest*

Love Your Enemies *by Sharon Salzberg and Robert Thurman*
The Book of Secrets *by Deepak Chopra*
The Ripple Effect *by Dr. Greg Wells*
Super Human *by Dave Asprey*
Becoming Supernatural *by Dr. Joe Dispenza*
Belong *by Radha Agrawal*

ACKNOWLEDGEMENTS

The most profound gratitude goes to life, my greatest coach and mentor. Life has imparted countless lessons and has also granted me happiness and the realization of my dreams.

I wish to convey my deepest appreciation to the exceptional individuals who have supported me and crossed paths with me throughout this incredible journey.

A heartfelt thank you is extended to my cherished daughter, Kamira Hase. Her unwavering love, intelligence, and constant support have illuminated my path during this writing adventure. I am eternally thankful for her encouragement and her unwavering presence and interest in my life. My gratitude also extends to my dear friend, Christina Middelberg, whom I've known since we were three years old. She has been my rock, offering not only emotional support but unwavering companionship, no matter how audacious my pursuits. Her love, strength, and support are a consistent source of comfort for me.

I offer my sincere admiration to the mentors and coaches who have played pivotal roles in my life. Sambodh Viram initiated my awakening and allowed me to see the world from a new perspective when I was 35 years old. His teachings on mindfulness, meditation, Reiki, healthy dietary choices, and yoga have been invaluable. Without his guidance and support,

I would not be where I am today. Many thanks to Sifu Wolfgang Herges, who introduced me to the DVD of "The Secret" by Rhonda Byrne and engaged in numerous discussions about this topic. This marked the beginning of my enlightenment and a profound understanding of the Law of Attraction and its interconnectedness. I express my gratitude to Rainya Dann, my hypnotist, who was the first to help me break free from stagnation and anxiety, guiding me toward a path of gratitude, transformation, and mindfulness. With her, I got to know my inner child and learned to take care of her. Rainya also introduced me to my new family, a new community of "Superheroes," where we all felt safe for the first time in 20 years.

Alexandra Cabane, my Tony Robbins results coach from Guatemala, possesses one of the kindest souls, and her energetic vibrations resonate perfectly with mine. She has been with me on this book-writing journey from day one, helping me overcome challenges related to deadlines and timelines, which often required me to practice patience when I was overly eager to share this project with the world.

My hope is that through this book, I can share the same inspiration that all of you have given me.

And don't forget: It's all connected.

ABOUT THE AUTHOR

For the past 25 years, Sara has been a visionary entrepreneur and executive in the advertising and corporate realms. Growing up in a multicultural environment, she faced numerous challenges at a young age when her parents separated, leading to her upbringing in two different countries. As a means of coping, she cultivated happiness and, unknowingly, manifested numerous remarkable achievements in her life.

Up to this point, she has moved a staggering 33 times, spanning continents, countries, and states. Armed with a master's degree in fine arts, she has excelled as an artist and a designer. In the fast-paced advertising industry, she thrived as a creative director while navigating the complexities of single motherhood. Building on her wealth of experiences, Sara then ventured into the corporate world, achieving remarkable success in establishing multiple companies. She has conducted numerous executive workshops on corporate branding and incorporated spiritual guidance as the cornerstone of successful design and business applications.

Over the past decade, Sara has experienced both highs and lows on personal and professional fronts. These experiences have led her to dedicate herself to understanding the art of manifesting and maintaining momentum after accomplishing goals. Along her journey, she has arrived at a simple conclusion: By embracing a positive mindset, elevating one's energy to its highest level, and aligning the body, mind, and soul, individuals can tap into the power of the Law of Attraction to lead lives filled with joy and abundance. Making a conscious choice to cultivate happiness daily will help maintain the momentum of positive manifestations.

Today, she has transitioned her career into motivational speaking and coaching. Her clients come from diverse backgrounds and aspire to break free from obstacles and discover simple solutions to ignite their transition to a positive mindset and live abundantly.

You can find out more about Sara, her courses, booking her to speak at an event, or sign up for her newsletter list at: www.SaraKissing.com

SAMPLE AFFIRMATIONS

- Every day, in every way, I am getting better and better.
- Every day, in every way, I am getting stronger and stronger.
- Every day, in every way, I am getting healthier and healthier.
- Every day, in every way, I am getting wealthier and wealthier.
- Every day, in every way, I am getting more and more beautiful.
- Every day, in every way, I am getting happier and happier.
- Every day, in every way, I am getting more and more relaxed.
- Every day, in every way, I feel more and more loved.
- Every day, in every way, I am getting _____ and _____.

AFFIRMATIONS FOR HEALTH:

- I am healthy and vibrant in mind, body, and spirit.
- My body is strong, and I treat it with love and care.
- I radiate energy and vitality every day.
- I am grateful for my good health and well-being.
- I nourish my body with wholesome foods and exercise.

- I am in perfect health and harmony.
- Every day, I am getting healthier and stronger.
- My body is a temple, and I honor it with self-care.
- I am the embodiment of health and wellness.
- I attract and manifest optimal health effortlessly.

AFFIRMATIONS FOR MONEY AND WEALTH:

- I am a magnet for abundance and prosperity.
- Money flows to me easily and effortlessly.
- I am open to receiving unlimited financial abundance.
- I am worthy of wealth and financial success.
- I attract opportunities to create wealth and abundance.
- I am aligned with the energy of abundance.
- Money comes to me from multiple sources.
- I am grateful for the abundance that flows into my life.
- I am a money magnet, attracting wealth in all areas.
- I am financially free and abundant.

AFFIRMATIONS FOR CONFIDENCE:

- I am confident and capable in all that I do.
- I believe in myself and my abilities.
- I radiate confidence and self-assurance.
- I am worthy of success and happiness.
- I embrace challenges with confidence and resilience.
- I am confident in expressing my true self.

- I trust my intuition and make confident decisions.
- I am fearless and unstoppable in pursuing my dreams.
- I am proud of who I am and what I have accomplished.
- I am confident in my unique gifts and talents.

AFFIRMATIONS FOR LOVE:

- I am deserving of love and receive it abundantly.
- Love surrounds me, and I attract loving relationships.
- I give and receive love unconditionally.
- I am worthy of deep and meaningful relationships.
- Love flows effortlessly into my life.
- I am a magnet for love and romance.
- I am loved and cherished for who I am.
- My heart is open to love, and I welcome it fully.
- I attract loving and supportive people into my life.
- Love is my natural state, and I radiate love to others.

AFFIRMATIONS FOR HAPPINESS:

- I choose happiness and joy in every moment.
- Happiness flows through me effortlessly.
- I deserve to be happy and embrace it fully.
- I find happiness in the simplest of things.
- My happiness comes from within and radiates outward.
- I am grateful for the abundance of happiness in my life.
- I release any negativity and invite happiness into my life.

- Happiness is my natural state of being.
- I attract positive experiences that bring me joy and happiness.
- Each day, I am creating a life filled with happiness and fulfillment.

AFFIRMATIONS FOR STRENGTH:

- I am strong, both mentally and physically.
- I possess the inner strength to overcome any challenge.
- My strength empowers me to face challenges with courage.
- I am resilient and capable of handling whatever comes my way.
- Strength flows through me, guiding me toward success.
- I embrace my inner strength and use it to create positive change.
- I am determined to achieve my goals and dreams.
- I find strength within and let it drive me forward.
- I am a strong warrior, ready to conquer any obstacle.
- My strength grows with each challenge I overcome.

AFFIRMATIONS FOR PARENTING:

- I am a loving and nurturing parent.
- I am patient and understanding with my child.
- I lead by example with kindness and respect.
- I listen to my child with attentiveness and empathy.
- I prioritize quality time and strong bonds.
- I empower my child to explore their passions.
- I discipline with compassion and understanding.
- I celebrate my child's achievements.

- I prioritize self-care for my own well-being.
- I cherish the journey of parenthood.

AFFIRMATIONS FOR PROFESSIONAL ENDEAVORS:

- I am destined to succeed in my career.
- I attract abundant opportunities for growth and achievement.
- I am confident and impactful in my field.
- Success is my natural state, and I have the power to be successful.
- I am open to learning and continuously improving in my profession.
- I deserve to be seen and recognized in my career.
- I am a magnet for prosperous collaborations and partnerships.
- I am focused, determined, and unstoppable in reaching my professional goals.
- Every day, in every way, I move closer to achieving my professional dreams.

NOTES

NOTES

NOTES

www.ingramcontent.com/pod-product-compliance
Lightning Source LLC
Chambersburg PA
CBHW050252010526
44107CB00003B/291